NEVER
ALONE

NEVER ALONE

Waking Up to Self-Love, Gratitude,
& the Whisper of the Infinite

JAX GOLDING

HOUNDSTOOTH
PRESS

COPYRIGHT © 2022 JACQUELINE GOLDING

NEVER ALONE
Waking Up to Self-Love, Gratitude, and the Whisper of the Infinite

ISBN   978-1-5445-3144-1   *Hardcover*

        978-1-5445-3145-8   *Paperback*

        978-1-5445-3146-5   *Ebook*

Contents

Dedicated to all those who believe and don't...may we all eventually understand the magick of the Universe, the love of the infinite, and that we are Never Alone.

Special mention to those who have travelled this epic journey with me and continue to do so. To my earth children, Gemma, Isabella, George, and Alfie, who break me down and raise me up, constantly teaching me lessons. To family, Scotty, and soul connections, my dearest friends, my soul tribe—you know who you are. To the lightworkers and healers to whom I've been led, thank you for your healing messages and guidance. Because of you, I remember that I'm a Violet Flame that bows to light alone, a soul incarnate. Divinity defined.

In it all, we are just leading each other home.

RAM DASS

Introduction

IT ALL BEGINS WITH THE BIRDS. SO MANY OUTSIDE MY BEDROOM window. Impossible to ignore.

Starlings perch upon every branch, it seems. Peculiar, with winter still hugging the southern hemisphere. The time is 4:00 a.m., maybe earlier. The chirping, relentless.

It's July 2020, and my son and I have been in Cape Town for five months already. A mere three weeks after our arrival, the South African president, Cyril Ramaphosa, announced a full lockdown with immediate effect. A new deadly virus is permeating the globe, and there's no time to waste. Without hesitation, Ramaphosa decisively decreed a hard lockdown to contain the uncontrollable and ravenous strain, which has already brought parts of Asia and Europe to their knees. Hospitals are overflowing and thousands are dying.

COVID-19. The pandemic forces the entire world to come to a grinding halt. The virus puts nations into submission, toppling them to their knees.

It's as if the Universe declares *enough is enough* and forces mankind to buckle under its might. Industries are shut with immediate effect. Where once there were plumes of smoke emanating from factory towers, now nothing. The skies can breathe again. Freeways and highways once jam-packed with traffic, now desolate. Mass production and consumption instantly halt as people live on less—far, far less—and begin appreciating more. We revert back to basics, spending quality time at home with our families, which we can no longer easily abandon because of life's stresses and everyday work responsibilities. The hamster wheel has abruptly stopped.

Choices and freedoms enjoyed all our lives, now revoked by nature, by all that was, and is, and always will be. The skies and oceans breathe again while the breath of life is extinguished from humans.

According to the World Health Organisation, COVID-19 was officially declared a pandemic in early March 2020, and here in July, more than 11 million cases have been identified and more than half a million people have lost their lives to the virus. Fear and panic permeate the world. And here I am, an ordinary single mum in extraordinary circumstances. Alone. Afraid. My anguished aching soul searching, seeking, and finally surrendering to the celestial magick and mysticism of the Universe.

Writing this now, I am humbled. I am grateful. I am in awe. For now, I see that which I was too blind to see before. I see Amazing

Grace. The birds, in fact, were a step toward that grace—toward new breath. Annoying as they were, they eventually woke me up, literally and metaphorically.

I will share more about this bizarre situation in the first chapter. The experience frames my awakening and how I now understand my life. I am loathe to use the term 'awakening' because it smacks of pretentiousness and the New Age garble of tree-hugging and love and light. My circumstances are dark, and even now, I try to move within the light but am acutely aware of my darkness and devilish ways. I do not suppress my demons, but rather, I acknowledge and work with them. For without darkness, there is no light; the two are interlinked and so is everything in life. There is no happy without sad, no good without bad, no yin without yang. Yes, those bloody birds woke me up for sure. Their chirping, cathartic. Their tweets, tantalising. Their song, serendipitous.

MY JOURNEY HERE

This is my fourth attempt at writing a book, my second attempt at this one. I always knew I would publish a book. And the time has finally come. Divine timing at play. This is a book about my life up until now. My early childhood and transition into adulthood, what framed my choices, and how my marriages collapsed. It explores my thought processes and how and why I still manage to squeeze the proverbial lemonade from lemons with a smile on my face.

In each iteration of this book, I was initially hell-bent on wanting to convey my pain—how things transpired and how I was conned. I wanted to highlight the insidious nature of my ex's addiction, but to villainize him in my memoir felt somewhat contrived. Stiff. Rigid. I certainly didn't want bitterness permeating the book.

I procrastinate putting pen to paper. The notion of being duped seems too easily packaged, too out of sync with the complexities of life and my personal journey. It fails to explore my inner twists and turns. Yes, my second marriage crumbled, but there is so much more to my story.

As I feverishly tap on the keys of my MacBook, I think of my journey here. There was a time I would have been ashamed to say I am twice divorced with kids by two different men. In my twenties, I remember remarking, 'Oh God, how can women have children with different men?' (Gulp, eye roll for effect.) And then came the infamous words: 'That will *never* be me.'

Now I'm *that* woman. And I'm finally able to say I'm unashamed. Yes, I am *that* person who birthed four beautiful souls—two girls and two boys—from two different men. I choose to not see my two marriages as failures in my life. I internalise the aftermath of the unions as life's precious gifts. Untidily and messily wrapped lessons. Are there remnants of guilt still hidden in the depths of my soul? Of course. I'm human after all, set up to believe in the wedding and the white picket fence. When things go awry with my kids or they lash out at me, I inadvertently blame myself for not giving them the traditional parenting setup. And yet, I have learnt to come back to the present, acknowledge the past, and not limit the future. It has taken me almost fifty years to get here.

Along the way, I chose a more tumultuous path to find freedom and joy. Rather than succumbing to societal norms and feeling caged, I've flapped away the stigmas which incessantly follow me like pesky flies from different familial corners or from some wives still clinging farcically to their own expired nuptials—gleefully excluding the divorcee from their dinner parties and sometimes even going as far as to exclude my children from playdates.

I recall JC's famous words: 'Forgive them for they know not what they do.' (I use JC to refer to Jesus Christ, as it makes him feel more accessible to me.) Crikey, let's be honest, I sure didn't know what I was doing. In hindsight, I question how the hell I ended up walking down the aisle, twice no less. As a little girl, I was hardly the type to role-play weddings, favouring bows and arrows and marbles instead.

I've always chosen, in my own small ways, to defy tradition and all conformities in an effort to forge ahead in an authentic manner. There is an Afrikaans saying, *Bo bont onder strond*, which translates to *Keeping up shiny appearances despite the shit underneath*. Many people I've known in this journey have chosen this route—keeping up appearances to secure their social status. Of course, these same people rarely have any real social standing to uphold. They simply want to save face amongst their peers, clasping desperately to small victories, proclaiming, 'At least I have a man' (*even if that man is an absolute arsehole*, I think quietly to myself).

I find that acquaintances, faux friends, or even family who live by this mantra dislike when I step out, when I choose to glow up in truth. They, in turn, opt to lowkey hate me or gossip about my 'tragic circumstance and unconventional waywardness.'

Still, I choose to openly expose my shit, dulling all remnants of gloss. Authenticity is freeing, and losing those who are not part of your tribe along the way is a worthy price to pay. My tapestry of choices—some good, some poor—are mine to make, and I own that. All along, I am exactly where I need to be. For that, I'm truly grateful.

AN INVITATION

If you're easily offended by the words 'fuck' or 'shit,' this book may not be for you. I fuck-fuck and shit-shit my way through a lot of life's curveballs. But if you can get past the language and put away some of your preconceptions of what a 'good life' is, I invite you to join me for a brief moment in time—as I share snapshots of my upbringing, my two marriages, and a plethora of experiences. My wish is that some of these experiences resonate with you and that some may even bring you laughter. Most of all, I want you to believe in hope and joy and love. I want you to embrace gratitude and love yourself like never before. Be open to the grace of it all.

So, here goes. Grab a tub of ice cream, a bag of crisps, a drink of your choice, a smoke, if you choose, or vape, if you do. Get cosy if it's cold in your part of the world. Relax in the sun if it's shining on you. There's nothing like a good ol' 'natter with a mate' as they'd say in Blighty or a *genegaap* (gossip) as they'd say in *die* Kaap. I'm about to spill the tea on me.

I'll do my best to be open and honest. To share about the vitriolic anger I felt in every fibre of my being. How I considered ending it all and may or may not have indulged in way too much booze and uppers. How I looked at the beautiful English Channel and wanted it to swallow me up, and why I didn't let it. What sisterhood and soul tribe mean to me. How the good shit still somehow outweighs the bad shit. Why I stand in gratitude for all of this. Why I feel my skirt is made from the embers of the ashes from which I rose, defiant, determined, and delighted at the glory and grace of life. Let my soul's hand clasp yours tightly as we ascend towards the light while still being grateful for the darkness. Namaste.

CHAPTER 1

Waking Up
in Cape Town

#freespirit

'And I can never be lost. I am a seed of greatness, descendent from a line of chiefs.'

Dr. Hohepa Tamehana

Alfie, my nine-year-old son and the youngest of four, is fast asleep. On the other side of the room, a handsome black Labrador and an insecure black and white Shih Tzu both stir and then settle again. Just two weeks ago, I could have never predicted a devastating pandemic would hit and force us into isolation. But here we are. I stare up at the blank ceiling, breathing softly, silently, and resign myself to the realities of being housebound.

We arrived in Cape Town weeks earlier. I came here to recover. I want to spend time with my eighty-four-year-old mother and hope my family will catch and comfort me in my fragile state. My second marriage has now crashed and burned. The animosity and emotional burden of years of abuse, finally catching up with me.

My ex dragged me through court (for a second time) mere weeks prior, accusing me of withholding contact, in an effort to exert control and secure residency in England. This, from the very man who refuses to financially support his son and makes zero effort to see him on prescribed days. Even though I already secured sole custody in our home country of South Africa with his consent, the dynamic of power and ego overtakes effective co-parenting.

I am tired from an arduous journey filled with court dates, social workers, abusive texts, and every inch of my dirty laundry laid bare in the cold court system for all to peruse. The custody battle catches me completely off guard. He needs help. I need healing. My son needs to know he is safe.

On top of all of this, I am dealing with the immense guilt of letting all my children down. They had a father figure, albeit flawed, and now they don't. My poor judgement rains down on me like unforgiving blows as I struggle in the boxing ring of life. The self-loathing supersedes everything. Yet again, I'm unable to keep my carefully orchestrated family unit together.

It doesn't help that the judicial system is now questioning my parenting ability. The patriarchal system was stacked against me from the start, and compassion falls by the wayside in favour of box-ticking. *Does she take him to school?* Tick. *Does he wear a coat when it's cold?* Tick. On and on it goes, and the pertinent questions seem to be left unasked. *Is there love? Is there safety?*

How burdensome it becomes to have to prove my worth over and over again. How challenging it becomes to try and expose emotional manipulation—the reams and reams of text messages are somehow never considered enough proof. Bizarrely, we robotically follow these laws which differ from country to country, all the while being emotionally battered and bruised. How skewed and misguided most of our societal practices are, and yet, we have to heed the rules—unquestioningly, like Davids who are not quite ready to sling the shot against the Goliaths of this world.

Finally, I've had enough. In conjunction with weekly therapy sessions, I seek help at an abuse centre. In the cold light of day, I look at the facilitator and admit I am abused. An ongoing occurrence for years. No physical scars evident but mental ones aplenty. All four of my children are undoubtedly impacted by the toxicity of it all. I'm beginning to say what needs to be said, but the peace I so desperately seek still remains a distant dream. Flashbacks of my own childhood and parents arguing pervade my head and the guilt gushes in. Speaking regularly to an abuse counsellor helps to keep me balanced and less fearful, and I'm now armed with effective life tools to tackle parts of my complex post-traumatic stress; I am finally able to be excited at the prospect of a new beginning.

BACK TO TOUCH DOWN
AND A FRESH START

When the Boeing 747 hits the tarmac of Cape Town International Airport on Valentine's Day 2020, I let out a big breath. It is as if something important is being released. A sigh of letting go. I just don't know what it is yet. About eight years earlier on this very day, I was on a yacht declaring my love and commitment to the man who becomes Alfie's father; my older children playing an integral part in the wedding ceremony. It is to be a new beginning for them as much as for me. A marriage that is supposed to instil hope that love can conquer all. A blended family by modern-day standards. I'm determined to give my kids a family with two parents. How had things taken such a turn since then?

I look over and see Alfie smiling wide. He claps his hands, exuberantly squealing, 'Can I swim when we get home?'

'A quick dip before we have to greet Ma,' I say, trying to keep an upbeat tone.

I usher us through customs, laden with our life squeezed into four suitcases. We meander our way through the airport to collect our rental car and drive to our own little sanctuary. A beautiful villa in a private security estate. I landed this gem of an unfurnished home virtually, a mere ten days prior.

My expectations of staying with family were shattered quickly after it was made blatantly clear by one member that our presence would create tension. Their large familial residences didn't have room for us. I am too outspoken and will fail to hold my tongue and sweep things under the rug, per the custom. I will scupper their Stepford wives existence, which spans private schools and hobnobbing with dignitaries, millionaires, billionaires, entrepreneurs, and politicians. They are used to keeping things *Bo bont onder strond*, and I, along with my gobby mouth, simply won't do.

As we pull up to the villa with its elaborate wrought iron gates and fingerprint access, it all sinks in. I'd moved us across the seas for peace and safety, but I won't receive support from my own flesh and blood. I will have no choice but to delve into what little reserves remain within. Oh, how tired I am of being so fucking strong all of the fucking time. Still, I know how to manage. I know how to do what I must. I stand resolute in front of the villa while feeling the burden of it all. The marble floors and high ceilings, closing in. A perfectly manicured lawn with a grandiose fountain and sparkling pool looking quite fetchingly back at me under the harsh sunlight.

I feel sad. Debilitating loneliness is creeping on in. I hand Alfie his swimming togs and faintly smile, giving him the thumbs up to jump into the much-anticipated swimming pool. He splashes about and cools himself in the suffocating heat. Goddammit, I need a cold drink. Oh wait, I have no fridge yet. This place is unfurnished. Another unplanned expense. Shit. Much still to do to make it fully our home.

Just weeks into our stay, the seriousness of the pandemic hits home. Its presence was not obvious on arriving, but now we realise its gravity. It's only us, a dynamic duo with our own secret handshake, our jet-lagged dogs, and an unknown entity encroaching ever closer on our enclave of enforced recuperation.

Two weeks into the pandemic, we still have no contact from my family. No calls. No including us in their bubble. As I gaze up at the ceiling in the early hours of that morning, I allow myself to feel the brokenness inside of me.

There will be no welcome home, no ticker tape parade of happiness. Nada from anyone with blood ties to me.

Not from my older brother, who has twins Alfie's age. Not from my mum, who lives next door to the parents of my brother's baby mamma. The families live in an exclusive area of Cape Town in a trio of houses. My youngest daughter (well, she's an adult in her early twenties) is residing with my mother as she enjoys an extended holiday in the comfort and opulence of family. My rented residence is on the other side of the mountain, a twenty to thirty-minute drive away.

Years and years of clamped-up sadness wells up. Bruised. Bereaved. Depleted. Disconnected. And the damn birds won't shut up. The windows are re-closed, the curtains drawn, and a pillow defiantly squished over my head. Still, their chirps and tweets are relentless. Unavoidable. Fuck the birds, fuck the ceiling, fuck family, fuck them all.

Then, just for a moment, I pause: *Why are these starlings here with such a sharp shrill. The sky is overcast, yet they continue to chirp. Storm clouds congregate overhead.* Then the answer: *They're announcing the beginning of spring. An internal renewal for me.* Sure enough, they were making an announcement. They were calling me to wake up. To breathe again. It's the heart of winter— the air chilly—yet they urge me to welcome a budding new season. Unexpectedly and urgently, they are calling on me to let the light into my dark desolate depths. Let *it* into the searing swirling sadness.

Ten weeks into lockdown, I find myself repeatedly waking up at 3:30 a.m., lying in bed, thinking, *What the fuck is happening?* I feel so alone, yet simultaneously serene and blessed.

My 'baby' boy and I are living each day at our own pace. In many ways, we are thriving and free. Blessed to be in a place of peace with comforts of our own making. Our favourite foods. Our best board games. We grow closer as each day passes, amusing ourselves through chats and jokes, books, running around the garden with the dogs, swimming in the pool, lying on cold tiled floors after being in the blistering African sun, screaming aloud as we drive around the mountain, and surfing together. We are learning to live again. Learning to embrace an attitude of gratitude.

My two closest Capetonian friends are our refuge—bringing candles and torches for those days that load shedding is scheduled. Load shedding is a common occurrence in South Africa when the electrical grid in your area is shut down for a couple of hours. My friends introduced us to the app Eskom se Push, which alerts us to the days and times, allowing enough time to download movies and get our snacks ready. Alfie and I love load shedding. When the lights cut out, the candles are lit, the fire is built, and books are taken out. Mind you, I have to learn to build a fire by watching countless YouTube videos. I try different methods from the pyramid stack to the inverted stack of wooden logs. I smoke out the lounge several times, but perseverance culminates in Alfie and I dancing with delight when I finally get it roaring on the third night. Lights flicker on the words in our books as quietness envelopes our happy home. What a blessing to have no internet. Our forced disconnection from it all leads to deeper connection—to mindful moments of NOW.

THE CALL

One night during load shedding, I wake, as usual, scanning the walls in the wee hours of the morning. *The grey cushioned headboard is not a bad choice for a bespoke queen size bed*, I muse. I consider how the furniture is competently arranged by a kind estate realtor named Anna. How blessed I am, having connected with Anna via WhatsApp while still in Brighton, England. She sources beds, a washing machine, crockery, and cutlery, and she even has milk, coffee, and miscellaneous bits at the ready on the day we land. Never before has a stranger blessed me like this.

I snuggle under the duvet. 'Ah, the grey striped duvet cover complements the headboard perfectly,' I whisper to myself. Truth is, I don't particularly like the bloody headboard, but it is cost-effective and works aesthetically. There is a lot to be thankful for, from Anna to our amazing landlord. It's like the Universe is throwing us Band-Aids of kindness.

I look over at the dogs. Both are snoring again. Rosie, the Shih Tzu, is in her typical position, curled up in Rolo's belly. Rolo's large lab paws outstretched across the teeny tiny dog bed. They could sleep anywhere, and this was their choice. Next to my bed, snoring and farting. Bloody ridiculous dogs, but you gotta love them.

I get up and walk across to the Juliette balcony, staring out the window at the night sky. I see the outline of the mountain across the horizon, from which I draw strength each day. The stars twinkle in the African sky, clear like a sumptuous black velvet throw.

Jax, you are seriously in shit, I chastise myself. *In a few hours you've gotta be up to homeschool Alfie, and maths is the first lesson of the bloody day. And you're shit at maths.* Then I remember I should be thankful that at least Alfie is in a wonderful school. His schooling is so vastly different from my own experience in the late seventies when South Africa was still firmly segregated under Apartheid and our student-to-teacher ratio was out of hand, facilities were poor, and education spending was tiered along racial lines.

All these random thoughts swirl in my head as I stare into the night sky. *Why am I so uneasy? It isn't really about maths, is it? Perhaps it's the stress of the second divorce or the remnants of the child access battle. Perhaps it's just me drinking too much water too close to bedtime.* I take yet another trip to the bathroom, placing my voluptuous arse squarely on the porcelain toilet seat as I stare at the mountain views and stars through the bathroom window. I think about how I picked up a few kilograms—the Covid couch potato bulge. *Thick thighs are a blessing*, I think. *They stop your cell phone from slipping into the bog.* Between the drip-drip and random thoughts, I feel something stir deep within me, reminding me of how the birds stirred me awake a few weeks before. Tonight is eerily different. Something in my gut tweaks. Not a bad tweak, more like a gentle tug. A pull.

I wash my hands and return to bed, but the land of Nod is elusive. DJ Duvet cannot lull me to sleep. That pull is subtly encouraging me to drag my butt downstairs into the garden. The time is now 3:40 a.m. The lazy lumbering lab stretches his long legs and rises with me. Rosie reluctantly follows suit, her flat face showing off her underbite quite severely in the moonlit room.

Two sets of brown eyes now look at me quizzically. I look quizzically at my yoga mat. We all move forward simultaneously. I snatch up the indigo yoga mat, and we ease our way downstairs, careful not to disturb Alfie. I roll out the mat in the darkness of the chilly winter morning, shooing the dogs to wee at the other end of the garden—not next to the damn mat. They show their confusion in their drowsy eyes and no wag in their tails. Why are they outside instead of in their doggie dreams? Indignantly, they do what they must before scampering back indoors.

Now I am alone. No neighbourly noises. Just the odd croak from a frog. As I stand beneath the moonlit sky, the stars overhead beckon me. The crisp winter air burns the inside of my nostrils. Stillness envelopes the moment. I set my bare feet on the cold, dewy grass and feel nothing. Do nothing. I simply stop. Stand. Still. Silent.

I gaze again at the morning sky, muddled smatterings of black and grey twinkling with the odd star burning bright. The sun slowly marching towards me, ready for the dawn of a new day. Still, I stand.

Then I let in the sound of the birds. This time, I'm not irritated at the noise. I simply witness the noise as I witness the sky's subtle symphony of changing colours. All still. Very still. I dare not move.

The cold blades of grass press under the balls of my feet, wet squishiness in between my toes. Not classic morning dew but rather icky sodden sand granules from last night's heavy downpour. I raise my arms towards the heavens, palms pressed together. Inhale, then exhale. Breathing in and out for God knows how long. My flimsy cotton pyjamas move quietly in the gentle morning wind. The air feels sacred. I'm not shitting you; it really does. And I'm not a God-botherer in any shape or form. But something in this moment is truly special. Majestic. Surreal. I throw my head back and stare vacantly into the blackness. The void.

And here, in a moment, I find what I'm seeking.

In truth, I don't find it at all; it finds me. I simply can no longer deny it. It has come. What? I don't know exactly. But it's here, inside of me, and it feels so damn good. So safe. So secure. So right. Is it God? Is it Source? Is it bliss? Is it pure peace? Perhaps all of those. I have no fucking clue.

Warm tears roll down my icy cheeks. They just keep falling. A trickle, then a cascade as I press my eyes shut. What the hell is happening? It isn't scary, but neither is it normal. I feel like I'm losing my marbles in a flow foreign to me. As if the feelings of being alone and abandoned are miraculously cleansed by salty tears. An utter sense of relief suddenly envelopes me. I lean into *it*. I embrace *it* and *it* holds me ever so tightly. The kind of hug I needed all my life but never got.

And then the words escape my lips. 'Thank you. Thank you,' I sob.

'Thank you for not forgetting me. And for bringing me home.' Gratitude permeates every fibre inside me. I drop to my knees, unbothered by the mud squelching around my legs.

I feel safe. So, so safe.

'Thank you, Universe. Thank you, Spirit,' I continue. 'Thank you, Source, the Divine, God, Cosmos, Spirit Guides, Ancestors, my Angels, and Spirit Animals.'

Avalanches of unapologetic tears continue. Soft utterances of simple thanks stream from my lips. The Akash in all its infinity reels inside me, outside me, above me, and around me. It's so hard to explain. SO hard to put into words. All simply *is*. The Alpha and Omega, the darkness and the light, the end and the beginning. And it feels right. I feel right. The moment is magical. Majestic.

I breathe in deeply. Peace.

I remember Rumi's words: 'That which I am seeking is seeking me.'

In this moment, Spirit is catapulting me through grief and darkness to love and light. I can finally accept all that is. I can give thanks for all pain and all joy. I can fully feel the breath of life bestowed on my earthly self.

Here in this moment, I can accept all forms of 'Source.' I've always struggled with the concept of God and how it translates from a church service into my everyday life. Why is the same God understood so differently by religions, and why does love not unite all religions into the same reverence for the same God. But here and now, the Universe somehow encapsulates my acceptance of God/Spirit and my belief in my Angels, my Spirit Guides, and my ancestors. It seems they have come to save me on this chilly winter's morning.

ANCESTRAL GRACE

The next day, a bit unsteady, I sat down to write and feel blocked. *Where do I go with this?* In typical me fashion, I grab my phone and scroll Instagram. The art of procrastination lies in Instagram. I love escaping through people's stories, laughing at their hilarious uploads, and being motivated by their strength and commitments. Especially during a time of lockdown, it is comforting to see how others are amusing themselves. As I scroll, I see a friend's niece uploaded a song. Not just any song. It feels like *the* song I need at just the right time. Its lyrics wax rhythmically into my soul. I lean into it as it touches my dark, damp, damaged depths.

The song is by Dr. Hohepa Tamehana, who is from New Zealand. It's called *He Kakano Ahau*, which translates to 'I am a seed.' Originally a Maori proverb, it reminds not only the Maori people but all of humanity of our rich ancestry. My soul's journey and mission—my dharma—become crystal clear. The call beckoning within my soul but muted by my stubbornness across decades is now trumpeting loudly. 'Spirit, I hear you,' I murmur as I weep. I understand.

Through the words of *He Kakano*, I am reminded I come from a great and powerful lineage and never walk alone. That I have walked across many lives and experiences. I can feel how my ancestors and Guides hold my hand and have my back. I acknowledge I'm a warrior born of greatness, given strength by Spirit to forge ahead. And with support from ancestors before me, whose knowledge I must draw on, I am steered to fulfil my purpose and heal my ancestry lineage.

The following are the lyrics from *He Kakano* (permission to share granted by Dr. Tamehana). I encourage you to listen to the song and let it move you.

He Kakano ahau
I ruia mai I Rangiatea
And I can never be lost
I am a seed born of greatness
Descended from a line of Chiefs

He kakano ahau
Ki hea ra au e hītekiteki ana
Ka mau tonu i ahau ōku tikanga
Tōku reo tōku ohooho, tōku reo tōku māpihi maurea
Tōku whakakai mārihi

My language is my strength, an ornament of grace
Ka tū ana ahau, ka ūhia au e ōku tīpuna
My pride I will show that you may know who I am
He morehu ahau
I am a warrior, a survivor

He Kakano ahau i ruia mai i Rangiātea
E kore au e ngaro
He kākano
Mai I Rangiātea
Mai I nga tīpuna, nga Rangatira
He kākano ahau

Ki hea ra au e hītekiteki ana ka mau tonu i ahau ōku tikanga
Tōku reo tōku ohooho, tōku reo tōku māpihi maurea
Tōku whakakai mārihi
He reo rangatira, he rākai ataahua

Ka tū ana ahau, ka ūhia au e ōku tīpuna
Ka tu kaha tonu ahau
Ki kite koutou, I tōku mana

He Kakano Ahau I ruia mai Rangiatea
And I can never be lost
I am a seed of greatness
Descendent from a line of chiefs
My language is my strength
An ornament of grace

DEEPER THOUGHTS BEHIND SOME OF THE LYRICS
directly from Dr Tamehana

He Kakano ahau i ruia mai i Rangiātea	*I am a seed sown from an ancient place.*
I can never be lost I am a seed born of greatness	*If we know who we are then we can never be lost*
Descended from a line of chiefs	*I believe that the people on the waka that travelled to Aotearoa were the best of the best. The best tohunga, navigators, warriors, breeders, and hunters. They were people of high ranking. Therefore, we are descended from people of status.*
Ki hea ra au e hītekiteki ana ka mau tonu i ahau ōku tikanga	*Where-ever I go I am Māori/ Tūhoe. This determines how I behave, react, or respond when engaging with the environment and those around me.*
Tōku reo tōku ohooho, tōku reo tōku māpihi maurea, tōku whakakai mārihi	*It is my language that awakens me, that keeps me connected to who I am as Māori/Tūhoe*
Ka tū ana ahau, ka ūhia au e ōku tīpuna	*My ancestors are always with me, they embrace me, they protect me, they guide me.*

I am a warrior, a survivor	*The Native Schools Act 1867 banned our language from being spoken in schools.* *The Tohunga Suppression Act 1907 banned our traditional healing practices.* *After everything Maori were subjected to, we have fought through it all. We are warriors, we are survivors.*

I include the complete Maori version to honour not only the language of the Maori but also that of all Indigenous peoples—from the Cherokee to the Cree from the Aborigine to the Amazonian, from the Khoisan to the Kallaway and *all* Indigenous cultures across the globe. The Spirit of our ancestors lives in us. It is time their wisdom is revered and their voices are heard. It is time we acknowledge our interconnectedness in all things.

TOTAL MAORI VERSION

He Kakano ahau i ruia mai i Rangiātea
E kore au e ngaro
He kākano
Mai I Rangiātea
Mai I nga tīpuna, nga Rangatira
He kākano ahau

Ki hea ra au e hītekiteki ana ka mau tonu i ahau ōku tikanga
Tōku reo tōku ohooho, tōku reo tōku māpihi maurea
Tōku whakakai mārihi
He reo rangatira, he rākai ataahua

Ka tū ana ahau, ka ūhia au e ōku tīpuna
Ka tu kaha tonu ahau
Ki kite koutou, I tōku mana

NOTE TO THE READER

The wake-up experience I had a few months into the pandemic truly shifted my understanding of myself and reality. It helped me accept and move on from my past perceived failures into freedom. In the following chapters, I will share in more detail my journey through life—as I moved in and out of places of awareness and ultimately to a place of healing. I'm forever grateful for all the highs and lows of my life and am now able to tell my story, knowing my language is my strength, an ornament of grace.

Rolo

Rosie

CHAPTER 2

∞

Arriving
in This World

#wednesdayvibes

'Out of suffering have emerged the strongest souls; the most massive characters are seared with scars.'

KHALIL GIBRAN

IT'S FITTING THAT I EXPERIENCE SUCH A DEEP REVELATION here in Cape Town, the same place I began my journey into this world.

I arrived as Jacqueline via caesarean section on an early Wednesday morning in October of 1971. No struggle involved and no squishy face, though Mamma always tells me I scarred her for life. The scar stretches across her belly below her navel from left to right as well as vertically. I don't think she's ever forgiven me for that.

I am the last born, a *laat lammetjie*. An unplanned pregnancy, arriving eleven years after my brother and nine years after my sister. According to my mother, my arrival ruined her plan of finally up and leaving my dominant, belligerent Dadda. Oh well, shit happens, and I am born. A Starseed soul incarnate to a father who had expected a son and wanted to call him George II and a mother who is more than just a bit fed up with her life.

The circumstances around my birth are not filled with excitement. My family carries on with the mundanity of life. That's how I understand it, at least. When I ask about my birth later in life, Mamma never elaborates, always stoically keeping things to herself. Dadda on the other hand is outspoken. In fact, too outspoken, explaining he wanted to call me Georgina, a commiseration name for not being born a boy. He explains he abandoned the idea since I 'didn't look the part.' What he's actually saying is that Georgina was a waste of bloody time. I am a girl, and he has to accept that there will be no male George the Second during his lifetime. Lucky for him, I will later give him the namesake in his grandson.

One of Mamma's favourite stories is of the time I won a baby competition. I was *not* the fairest of them all, no, but I WAS crowned the healthiest of them all. During the seventies, healthy was *rond en gesond*, or 'round as a pound.' In truth, I was fat with seven rolls on my arms and multiple folds on my chubby legs.

Chubby for the win with prized food hamper

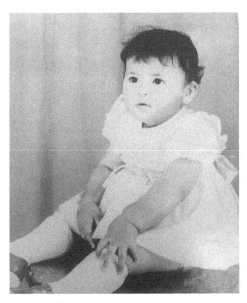

Sitting pretty in innocence

And what did I win? A large hamper of bloody food. Mamma also likes to boast that at three months old, I was being supplemented with condensed milk mixed with water (obviously cooled boiled water). She claims she wanted to feed my sweet tooth. 'At three months, am I still not all gums?' I ask her. She ignores the question. This sweet dietary supplement apparently is what secured the win at said baby competition. It's a miracle that I have a gleaming white smile of permanent teeth having never seen the inside of a dentist until I became a working woman who could afford to foot the bill.

EARLIEST MEMORIES

I am raised in the Cape Flats, postcode 7764. This is a vast area in Cape Town, South Africa where 'Coloured' people were forcibly relocated during the Group Areas Act, which was put in place to separate white residential areas from those who were racially grouped as Indian, Black, Coloured, or mixed race. Coloured was a term to define, I suppose, a hue of blackness. During the Apartheid years, it was considered a vulgar term, but in recent years, people in the community have owned the term to define their own particular heritage. I suppose it is now an identity, which is a mix of ethnicities and inter-racial components.

To segregate people, a ludicrous method called the pencil test was used, unless the race was blatantly obvious through skin colour or facial features. In this test, a pencil was placed in the hair. If it slid out, you were racially defined as white. If it did not, then you were clearly not white according to the Apartheid powers that be.

The conundrum was which category to slot my diverse parents' arses into. Mother, having obvious Asian features with sleek hair, and Father, probably much more easily classified because of his afro hair. Ultimately, they were both classified as Coloured.

Many families were split up during this time. Our own family, I recall my father saying, was divided. He spoke vaguely of knowing of two brothers with their own families. One brother who was fair was regarded as white or at least he could 'play white,' as people on the Cape Flats would disparagingly remark. The other darker-skinned sibling was classified Coloured.

Generations later, racially divided families led separate lives based on privilege or lack thereof. Black communities were renowned for being more welcoming of other races into the community, and mixed-race children born from 'illegal' relations between white and Black lovers could happily thrive in these enclaves of diversity. These children could happily live in a community where neighbours were at least accepting of them some of the time.

My own neighbourhood growing up was classified Coloured and had a rich tapestry of extended family relations, as opposed to white neighbourhoods, which were simply white.

My father was a chiropodist; my mother, an aspiring nurse. The closest she got to realising her dream was to volunteer at the Salvation Army. During my earliest years of life, her daily grind was working in a local factory, dutifully handing her weekly monies over to my father. When I started primary school at six years of age, she opted to help out in a family friend's fish shop to earn money to help support the family.

Her kids were both her world and her prison. Mamma was an emotionally detached mother, harbouring her own trauma, but she fulfilled all requirements needed for competent childcare. She kept us clean, fed, and well mannered. Her mantra was that children should be seen and not heard. She valued her marriage and the respectability that came with having children and a house she could call her own. She was as independent as she could be within the confines of a sixties marriage. I remember being told stories of how she would happily nip around in her powder blue Mini Cooper. She was proud of the fleet of cars Dadda drove, from a black Jaguar with red leather seats that smelled new to a red Valiant and a beige Colt Galant. She often recalls that they were posh enough to own a three-wheeled BMW in their early days of courtship.

Mamma, like me, saw herself as happy until, well, she wasn't. From as early as I can remember, I felt the tension in the marriage. I noticed during my teenage years that it was certainly not an equal partnership. There was no love between my parents. Yet, they needed each other. Mamma often declared to me that she would be a merry widow. Dadda seemed to regard her as a merciless nag, and she considered him a burden. The truth was that Mamma was emotionally battered and bruised while Dadda was insecure and depressed. Simply put, they were co-dependent in the worst ways. As their youngest child, I was the glue that held them together and compelled them to fulfil their responsibility of raising me—together.

By six years old, I had a lisp and would often be called out to perform in front of visitors or family whenever needed. 'One, two, three, four, five, tix.' Yes, I couldn't say six—S's and J's eluded me. 'Go on, Jacqueline, recite Janet and John,' said one neighbour invited over for a cup of tea. Up I would get without catching on to why I was asked to re-enact my verbal inadequacies. I just believed I was bloody brilliant. Kudos to me for being blind to it all, believing in my own perceived precocious brilliance. It was worth the tiny Pick & Mix choccy reward.

In fact, I found it empowering as I breathed deep, looked guests in the eye, and loudly exclaimed, 'Danet and Dohn' and heard the raucous laughter and comments. 'She's so cute,' said one bespectacled lady with mauve hair. 'Aaaah, if she were mine, I'd have her wake up and count for me every damn day,' said another rather rotund aunt in her floral dress and tightly curled hair with bright red lipstick matching the overstretched roses. 'Go on, my dear, count again ending off with Janet and John.' She fiddled with her fake pearls, strung snugly around her double-chinned neck and stared intently at my round face and little hands clasped tightly together.

It was decided that when I started at primary school I would be called Jackie. Far easier to learn to write than Jacqueline. This wouldn't be my final name change. I would later go by Jacquie (as a young adult) and Jax (post-divorce). My surname would also be double-barrelled during marriage number one, as I hitched my surname to my husband's and placed a defining dash between the two. Double barrelling was all the rage in the mid-nineties. When I married again, I simply refused to take another surname and held on to my own Jewish-sounding one. Far more intriguing for a brown-skinned girl to have a Jewish name and then pop up in an interview looking the way that I do, with Asian-shaped brown eyes and racially defined as Coloured. The interviewers fumbling with questions as they re-checked my surname never ceased to amuse me.

Name changing has been like shedding a skin for me. A new name or variation thereof allowed for fresh beginnings. A new me. A different me. Or so I believed. In hindsight, it was me with the same baggage. The little girl, still trying to be validated in a different skin of a name. I hoped that this new present-day version of my now 'grown-up' name of Jax would allow me to finally carve out an iota of value for myself without my worth being intertwined with performing well or pleasing others.

By the time I entered primary school at six years old, I had already realised which parts of me were acceptable and which were not. I walked to school on my own or with an older kid from down the road. It was a mere fifteen-minute walk. School was easy for me, both socially and academically. I was often praised for coming first in class. 'Jackie, well done, you have my brains.' An odd but frequent statement from Dadda, who also took credit for my thick hair, claiming I was the reason he was bald. Go figure. Mamma would just roll her eyes, recognising how his need for acknowledgement encroached even on my little triumph of being top of the class. School reports sang praise, and I lapped it all up. So did Dadda.

Mamma would haphazardly clear away the plates, clanging and banging them in the sink as she mumbled under her breath. 'Yes, yes, George, you gave her everything. I only just got sliced open.' At this point, I would silently grab the chequered red-and-white drying cloth and silently and obediently dry the dishes while Dadda snapped open his broadsheet newspaper and burrowed his bespectacled face into the headline news.

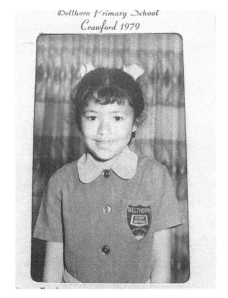

The Seventies

Precocious, obedient and compliant

MASKS AND MAYHEM

Of course, I learnt the masks I needed to wear to survive in the world soon enough. Excelling academically was the only way to receive praise and acknowledgement, be it from my parents or eldest and only brother—my Boeta.

My brother's shadow affected me more than anything. His only interest in me was my academic performance. When I was seven, he gifted me my first book: *Darwin's Evolution*. I used to observe my Boeta closely and noticed he hardly had a relationship with my father. Often left to his own devices from a young age, he enjoyed many privileges as the only male offspring from parents who were usually very strict. An aspiring footballer, he had accumulated loads of trophies before I was born. Mamma would diligently polish them and leave them in the hallway showcase for all to see. Neither Mamma nor Dadda attended a single one of his football matches. Still, my parents seemed to adore my brother. He was the apple of my Mamma's eye, even into adulthood. And my father adored having a son so much that he would take him to work in a cardboard box to show him off to his patients. Taking your son to work was quite a progressive move in the sixties.

My brother was in his twenties by the time I was ten years old. I remember he gave me *Iron Heel* by Trotsky. He was a socialist back then. (It's strange that now in his sixties he is a fully fledged capitalist with philanthropic outreaches.) I never actually read the book, opting for Archie comics instead. Jughead triumphs over Trotsky all day, every day when you are ten years old.

Still, my self-worth was undoubtedly woven into what I observed about my brother and how he was acknowledged. I naturally linked my worth to what I achieved. I was top of my primary school classes for four solid years before slipping into second place. End of term, my name was always called to receive a book prize or a certificate. After year two, my parents couldn't be bothered to attend a parents' evening or prize presentation, as it was a given I would trump everyone. Still, when I slipped to second place, I was devastated. All my worth was etched into those little prized trophies and books. It meant everything for my name to be mentioned as I twirled my two pigtails and proudly walked in my starched uniform to receive the certificate, even if my parents weren't anywhere to be found. My young mind was already fully trained to see my value intertwined with accolades.

Moulded by Merits

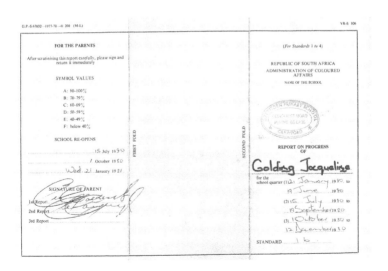

NEVER ALONE

40

Whilst at primary school, I wasn't allowed to play with the other kids in the street. I was limited to our backyard where friends could come to visit. If tennis balls flew over the wall, my mother would be enraged. '*Blerrie* hooligans. Why must they play in the street?' I would cringe but somehow always managed to maintain a relationship with all those kids. They'd often curiously ask, 'Why can't you *jus somme* come out, huh?'

'Ag, because my parents won't let me, you know.'

'That's not nice, hey, but it's awright. Next time, neh?'

'Ja, next time.'

Neither being scholar patrol nor a prefect (which is an accolade awarded to a select few senior pupils empowered to monitor behaviour and, hopefully, report the breaking of school rules such as untidy uniforms) at primary school would make my parents budge on allowing me to play beyond the bloody yard. But when Mamma was not looking, I would chat with the kids through the gate, my face pressed against the fence as they bounced the ball trying to include me. If they were caught, Mamma would undoubtedly scold them, and I would get a smack. No timeout. My parents opted for a good old-fashioned spanking, favouring the old-fashioned saying, *Spare the rod, spoil the child.* In their view, it did neither me nor my siblings any harm and instilled respect. While my father would simply yell, my mother would opt to use her wooden clog which, from experience, I can share that a beating with a wooden clog is by far more painful than a bloody bamboo cane used often by my teachers at school.

I gathered my street smarts early in secondary/high school, enjoying the privileges of being a prefect but obviously never ever reporting anyone—because that would simply be stupid if you attended a state school. The power of prefect duty is immense and useful in gaining popularity amongst your peers when used correctly. An example of this would be to alert smoking students when an actual teacher was approaching and fumbling around said teacher saying you just cannot seem to detect from which exact cubicle the nicotine smell is emanating.

TEEN YEARS AND RACIAL IDENTITY

My entrance into the teen years was with the only birthday I ever celebrated—my crown. I would turn thirteen on the thirteenth day of October. I'd never had a birthday party before, as my parents considered it a waste of money. My sister oversaw it, and I had friends, a cream cake with actual candles, and music playing from the cassette tape. My parents were nowhere in sight, out to escape it all. I was ecstatic. It is one of the fondest memories I have of my fun-filled teenage years.

Those were the years with no iPads, no cell phones, only VHS, boom boxes, and a Sony Walkman with foam earphones *if* you were cool. Ah, the eighties. The era of rap music, roller skates, Madonna, Mariah Carey, Brenda Fassie, and Whitney as well as NWA, Ice Cube, Snoop, Bayete, Juluka, Johnny Clegg, Lucky Dube, and Tina Turner.

My whole world was bigger in high school. By thirteen, catching the bus to school was the norm, and glorious freedom was fervently welcomed. I effortlessly made friends. I was studious but also fun-loving. Always one of the boys but not to the exclusion of the girls. I could easily morph from one group to the next.

Some of the boys were fuck boys and were happy to share their conquest details with me. It was hanging out with the lads that probably deterred me from having sex at all during high school. My reputation was far more valuable. And I was streetwise enough to know that intimacy would not be kept between us. It didn't matter that there weren't even cell phones in those days. Word got around. Besides, my parents would kick the shit outta me, and I didn't think of it as a 'fun' thing to do.

Sex was synonymous with pregnancy in my mind. I had no clue about condoms. And frankly, the sex = pregnancy belief rang true, as several friends did, in fact, fall pregnant, which led to gossip, and this is where you either remained friends with them or left them out in the cold. Friendships to me were far more valuable, so those who did fall pregnant remain my friends today.

I may not have been sexually active myself nor a user of drugs, but let's just say my circle of friends was wide and varied and dipping into all sorts during high school. On the occasions I wanted to party, I crossed my legs and spread only my angelic wings, removing my halo to take several swigs of alcohol. I knew how to have fun, with vodka being the preferred drink of choice and countless snogging marathons. My kissing conquests duly noted on my Care Bear poster stuck against my bedroom door.

I was competent at sports, neither brilliant nor useless (a safe middle-of-the-road type of teammate) and was active in the

SRC (Students Representative Council), a student body responsible for organising awareness programmes during the eighties. I started high school during the final struggle years, where the disadvantaged were still fighting for the unbanning of the African National Congress and the freeing of Nelson Rolihlahla Mandela, Ahmed Kathrada, and Walter Sisulu, among other political prisoners. During my first year at high school in 1985 and my final year in 1989, there was political unrest and school-going pupils were fully engaged in political activities in Cape Town. The entire country was a fireball of human protests.

At thirteen years old, I was holding placards during protests. A typical school day involved teachers allowing time during class for political feedback to fellow pupils. During this time, they would outline protocols that would be used during demonstrations planned for the next day or week.

My first high school was adjacent to a police station. It was illegal to host peaceful demonstrations even if it was simply holding a placard from within school premises and against the wire fence reading 'Unban the ANC.' We'd hold it there so passing vehicles and commuters could read it, hoot, or raise their fists in solidarity. One day after our demonstrations, the police charged in with tear gas and sjamboks—a stiff long whip that was a South African weapon of choice (my father had several). We had to hide under the desks during the rampage of beatings.

Both my parents were very supportive, and regular school lessons were forgone for mass rallies instead. 'Far more educational,' said Dadda. My father was a very charming 'people person' who was proud of his family and his achievements, despite the racial challenges he had undoubtedly faced. Being a young man of mixed race, he was feisty and determined to not be boxed in.

Often when travelling on public transport, as a Black adult male, he was assigned seats for Non-whites. If there were empty seats, and they were marked 'Whites Only,' Dadda had to stand. When using public toilets, the same rule applied. Every encounter he had had with white people was degrading. To them, he was not a loved father nor a respected chiropodist. He was simply a Coloured man who had to know his place in society. He was nothing.

Dreams and hopes of a young Dadda

He vented his resentment towards whites by yelling 'at' them when they appeared on the telly. He revered heavy-weight boxing champion Muhammed Ali for his truth bombs about the white man. Dadda thrived on Ali's boxing matches, particularly the one in 1975 when he fought Chuck Wepner. I was four years old and remember Dadda listening to it on the radio. To Dadda, any victory he witnessed by Black people over white people made him proud.

He taught me about Black power and raising my clenched fists. His favourite saying was, 'The whites will be chased to the sea.' It gave him comfort to know that change was afoot in the country. The erosion of his self-worth as a young male during everyday encounters took its toll at times, and when he felt powerless outside the home, he exerted dominance inside it, which was unpleasant for us all.

During my high school years, many mass rallies were held. Hundreds and sometimes thousands of people would attend to hear political speeches about the future of the country. There was a palatable change in the nation: in schools, churches, mosques, and wherever people were willing to gather and listen. I remember asking my parents' permission to attend a political meeting, which would require taking a train to listen to a banned speaker. I wouldn't be attending school that day but knew the onus was on me to complete any outstanding academic work. My parents said a prayer and sent me off with a wave. Missing school in favour of a more fruitful education was a common occurrence.

That day I learnt how to make a petrol bomb and how to cover my face with the obligatory PLO red check scarf to protect against tear gas smoke being hurled among us students by the police. My mates and I ran for our lives as the *sjamboks* came out with pursuing police, followed by the dreaded rubber bullets and water cannons. And then there was the excruciatingly painful blow to the head from a brick that my friend decided to hurl from a moving train. As soon as I stood up, I collapsed. His aim was a bit off, but he still managed to hurl another at a police car, hitting the target and smashing the windscreen. I later got a head rub, a nudge, and a pat on the shoulder. 'At least you fell inside the train and didn't topple out,' he said. Raucous laughter followed.

Four years later, I switched schools because I needed to pass both mathematics and physics in order to attend university. And I was shit at both. I've always been more of a creative. English and languages were my jam. So physics had to go, and the only way to drop it was to attend a completely different school that would allow me to take history instead. This school was situated in Athlone, and it was near here that the world would witness a tragedy of epic proportions—since known as the Trojan Horse Massacre.

The murders occurred two days after my fourteenth birthday. The railway and security police worked together to crush a demonstration by the youth. A railway truck was loaded with crates, but behind these crates, armed police hid. The truck manoeuvred into the crowds and the police opened fire, injuring several youngsters and murdering three: ages twenty-one, fifteen, and eleven. None of the thirteen police were ever prosecuted.

The protesters were only armed with stones while the police had bullets. To this day, I will never forget the packed streets as we all mourned the loss and walked hand in hand. People united and fired AKs and Kalashnikovs from bakkies to show rage at the senseless murders. At home, we had nighttime vigils. Neighbourhoods united in shock and anger, in grief and defiance, knowing it could have been anyone's child. Dadda's response was succinct: 'The police are pigs.'

NAVIGATING ADOLESCENCE

The rest of my teenage experience was balanced between being a model student and turning a blind eye to my friends lighting up their cigarettes decked out in full school uniform and blazer, no less, at the back of the bus. I was adept at balancing expected responsibility and a level of street smarts. I attended countless house parties, regularly went to watch break dancing in the local park, and attended fairgrounds, which was the local fair that rolled into town once a year. It was the highlight for us teenagers, and we brimmed with excitement when it arrived. On the days that the fairground was set up, usually for at least three days, I could stay out all day and night riding on high swings, eating candy floss, and hopefully, holding hands with someone I fancied.

The truth was, my friends and I often had to entertain ourselves. I kissed a boy I utterly adored at seventeen and danced till my 11:00 p.m. curfew any chance I had. I'd walk the streets with my clique of ten, usually an even number of boys and girls. If we were not at someone's house, we frequented public parks or spaces where we played loud music, drank, and laughed.

On one occasion, a girlfriend got so drunk that we had to struggle home onboard a bus, an arduous forty-minute journey. On arrival at our stop, we fumbled out of the bus, walked two blocks, politely dumped her on the front lawn of her house, knocked on the door, and ran off.

My parents were wise when it came to handling me and alcohol. I think they chose to turn a blind eye since I excelled academically and was not sexually active. I remember one particular incident vividly. I had played truant to drink at my best friend's house and to see boys. In my drunken state, I ended up coming home with a fully fledged public road stop sign—the entire bloody sign—and triumphantly propped it in my room. Neither one of my parents blinked an eye. I puked that evening in the loo adjacent to their bedroom. Still not a murmur from them.

I had many adventures like this. One time, a bestie and I polished off her dad's brandy and whiskey. We baked a very rich chocolate cake and consumed it, only to regurgitate it all over the house. Another time, I climbed through windows with girlfriends, after sneaking out of their houses, only to be caught by snarling mothers waiting patiently on the other side of said window. I drag raced in cars, was chased by the police during one wild night, celebrated poppa wheelies and wheel spins, drank too much vodka and Southern Comfort, and ate too many Gatsbys (a local junk food eaten on the Cape Flats—it's a large loaf of bread stuffed with *slap chips* or fried potatoes that would usually accompany a portion of fish and chips, but in a Gatsby, you replace the fish with meat or *polony* and make it as spicy as possible).

At the end of each high school year, I'd have a *braai* with friends, but because of Apartheid, only certain areas were available to Coloured kids and only certain beaches were open. Same with cinemas. By my final year in high school, I was at the club every night of the week, without my parents ever knowing. Somehow, I still managed to get into university with an exemption. Not a bad feat for someone who partied like there was no tomorrow. And yet, comparatively speaking, I was the tame one in my group of friends.

Although I was streetwise, footloose, and free in some respects, I ultimately garnered my sense of worth through what I could do for others. I felt worthy when acknowledged but also felt good if I could make someone else smile. It gave me a sense of making a difference because, after all, kindness doesn't cost a damn thing, does it? However, the lines became blurred between being of service to others and people-pleasing. This pattern would ultimately lead me towards an adulthood of ingrained and conditioned behaviour, repeatedly reenacting what I knew.

Despite being reasonably happy during my teenage years, home life was full of tension. My older siblings had moved out, so I was often the only witness to the mighty blowouts between Mamma and Dadda. One day, after a particularly brutal fight, Mamma went outside, tired of the domineering and emotional cruelty of her husband. 'Being treated like a dog means I will be a dog,' she said, and she curled herself into a ball where the dogs would lie on the *stoep*. Oh, how I hated Dadda at that moment. Hated him with all my might. I vowed that I would never let a man trap and abuse me because of being financially dependent.

Mamma eventually went inside, and the next day, all was deathly silent. Dadda stepped lightly, and Mamma cooked him snoek, a favoured local fish.

CAREER WOMAN

University was a blur, fuelled by endless partying, to be honest. I started smoking cigarettes; I drank, danced, and had my first sexual partner. I excelled in the bedroom but performed poorly academically and eventually ended up changing cities and working briefly as a credit controller for a TV company before being enrolled in a journalism cadet course, propelling me into a writing career. Again, I transformed my name slightly to Jacquie once I became a career woman. Another shedding of a skin. A new phase in my life. As far as I was concerned, this next chapter demanded a name that fit my new journey as a cub reporter with a byline. In my mind, Jacquie was a bit more intriguing and a suitable compromise for Jacqueline. Also, it looked far more polished than Jackie, which was often pronounced *Jecki* on the Cape Flats.

I was enrolled as an intern at a prestigious newspaper in Johannesburg. It was 1992, and I was working at a pub by night and learning shorthand and how to touch-type on a computer by day. Yep, learning shorthand squiggles lets you know how bloody old I really am. The newspaper was an independent tabloid reporting impartially in a country that clamped down on freedom of speech. The realities of Apartheid South Africa were still in full swing. My mentors at the newspaper were veteran reporters and editors from whom I learnt much. I was the youngest in the newsroom, celebrating my twenty-first birthday with my peers a year on.

I earned my monetary tips at the Yard of Ale, a local bar and restaurant, serving the who's who of Jozi. Ironically, the locals who hung out at this establishment represented the emerging new diverse South Africa. Many would, in the years to come, become famous in diverse fields from entertainment to politics. For now, we would simply enjoy drinks together celebrating the changes afoot. The establishment I worked for represented an integrated environment of different creeds and cultures, and I thrived.

By this point, I had bought my first car. Dadda had loaned me 500 rands which is the South African currency. I was a confident young woman who drove herself to work now in my blue and white Budja Bug with a sticker of Bart Simpson showing his arse at the rear. The brakes were always failing, resulting in many missed crashes and one minor accident with an SUV. Luckily for me, it occurred right outside a police station on my way to work at a busy intersection. I was looking particularly cute that day and mustered all my street smarts to ensure a small settlement was paid in instalments. Fortunately for me, the police officer taking my statement was not white, which helped matters. My dislike for the police was momentarily put on hold as I smiled and pled ignorance at how the brakes failed.

I eventually graduated to front of house at the pub, and my meagre salary helped with paying repair bills for relentless oil leaks and a sticky clutch. The noise from my little second-hand vehicle was deafening, and the exposed engine heralded my departure and arrival home to a block of flats in Yeoville. Fortunately, I lived in an apartment my brother owned, so the financial reliance and allegiance was fortified. The price I paid for staying in his flat did compromise my own integrity when he asked me to lie for him as he juggled several women. I thought them foolish to hang on and be so dependent on his validation, yet I was blind to my own lack of self-worth and dependency.

As Jacquie, I was confident, people-loving, and hardworking. However, there was still no self-love. I didn't fully comprehend what self-love was. To many, self-love is having a spa day or having their nails and hair done, and I did all those things regularly in my twenties. Let's just say, these were essential budgetary requirements, alongside cigarettes. But as I now know, self-love is so much more than that. I would go so far as to say that true self-love is only understood when we have gone to the depths of our darkest crevices of crazy and faced our deadly demons, as painful as that may be. Only then does self-love eventually bloom. Like a lotus emerging from the mud.

Self-love doesn't come like a quick fix. It doesn't show up overnight. It is forged through relentless purging, sobbing, screaming, self-hatred, self-criticism, anger, and all the bandwidths of emotion. You can only know self-love if you know what self-hate is. Over time, I would come to realise that only I could love me as much as I yearned to be loved. The problem was that I didn't know I had to fill my own cup first until it spilled over, before engaging in romantic love. I didn't realise others could break me if I didn't have strong boundaries first. I could not comprehend a love towards myself or even where to start with that process, and so the abusive cycle began.

The more I gave to the wrong people, the more my worth was wrapped up in needing their attention. I desperately needed to be acknowledged because not being seen meant I was unworthy and unloved. Or so I thought. A fear of abandonment would creep up, and my ego would not accept being left out in the cold. So greater efforts would be employed to please and hold on to those I loved. Whether or not that love was reciprocated. It didn't matter.

Throughout my twenties, thirties, and forties, I wore the 'fix-it cum nurturer cum people-pleasing' cloak of unworthiness and neediness in all my relationships with others. Some people were kind and generous and worthy of my energy. Others, not so much. Ironically, those who were the most loyal demanded the least from me while others extracted as much as they could without reciprocation.

Since I never felt protected or valued, I chose emotionally unavailable men. Then married them. I easily remedied matters by compartmentalising. I could meticulously build an illusion of these men as those who took care of me and made me feel safe. Ridiculous, I know, but hindsight always provides 20/20 vision. Even that statement makes me crack up laughing at how the Universe works—20/20 vision. Shit sure hit the global fan in 2020, and everyone got to reflect on their life. For years, we have been using the saying '20/20 vision' without knowing what an enlightening manifestation 2020 would actually be.

When I reflect, I see my patterns with some clarity. I remember the first serious relationship where I caught the feels. I met him in a club. In those days, there was no Tinder, Hinge, or Bumble, so nightclub it was. He called me the next day, talking about our slow dance the night before. He was kind, and soon I met his mum and brother. A lovely family living in Mitchells Plain in Cape Town. Everything seemed great until I realised how bad his mandrax addiction was. He eventually spent time in prison and came out worse than when he went in. I was only nineteen years old when that relationship began, and my parents sent me to live in another city, fearing I would run off, convert to Islam, and get married. Frankly, I was considering all of that. He was one of the kindest, most genuine people I ever met, but his demons kept him in the depths of despair. I tried to fix it all for him, naively failing to understand that this was his journey to navigate.

I honoured aspects of his religion because of his dedication to prayer five times a day. I saw that when he adhered to his faith, things would improve. Devotion helped, but ultimately it was clear what choice he would make. He chose the drugs. His duality was plain for me to see, and despite our loving journey together, we parted ways. I in one city, he in another. He died a couple of years later, his baby mamma tracking me down and calling me to let me know.

To dull the heartbreak, I continued to chip away fervently at my career. However, my experience with his religion would plague me for many decades to come. I felt overwhelmed by the complexity of mainstream religion and wondered why I didn't feel a fervent urge to belong to any of it. I was drawn to the idea of a globally united vision, and years later I would be drawn to Hinduism and aspects of Zen and a plethora of other religions such as the mysticism of Kabbalah. Yet, I never subscribed to any particular religion, instead, finding comfort in different strands during different phases of my life. Even at this young age, I believed in something greater but could not pinpoint it. So, I focused on work.

At twenty-one, I was thriving as a reporter and had a new boyfriend. This guy had no drug addiction, but he harboured dark narcissistic tendencies. However, I was in love. His troubled background made us an odd pair to outsiders as I seemed to have it somewhat together in my own life.

'Where were you today, Jacquie?' I remember him asking one night. 'You came home ten minutes late. Where the fuck were you?'

'I dropped a girlfriend at home,' I said, placing the freshly cooked meal in front of him. He had watched me cook and not said a word till now.

'You fucking what? Dropped a girlfriend at home? Did you now! And I had to wait for my food?' Before I knew it, the plate was hurled against the opposite wall. Spaghetti splattered like blood-ied brains, tomato and garlic pasta sauce smeared chunkily against the whitewashed walls. I quietly got a cloth and began cleaning it up. After all, the place was rented, and I had paid the deposit.

This relationship ruled my life. I knew that. I was a journalist by day, doormat by night. No one would ever suspect. I constantly made excuses for him. His dysfunctional upbringing. His low self-esteem. His need to be loved. Ironically, I couldn't see what was right in front of me. Had I taken a breath, just for a moment to reflect inward, I would have seen that the guy I was trying to save did not need saving; it was *I* who really needed it. I enjoyed saving him so much that I didn't know how to save myself. I was a functioning dysfunctional woman still adept at wearing a mask. Easily able to perform as I did at six years of age to make others feel better. I could lift them up emotionally, but it was I who needed to be uplifted.

The last straw in this new relationship came when I had to house-sit my friend's luscious apartment. It had large bay windows and beautiful white shutters. She had exquisite taste in lounge chairs, boasting textured, colourful cushions and matching throws. It was an opportunity for respite from the daily emotional abuse, which I was now eight months into. But as I packed a few items of clothing, having given my boyfriend a heads-up about a week earlier, I sensed him watching me. He was irate, yet holding back. I could see the vein throbbing in his neck, the restless tapping of his fingers.

Abuse survivors know you always, always give notice of your plans. No surprises are ever welcome. And as I put the last sweater in my overnight bag, with his eyes peering into the back of my head, I said, 'I'm off, will see you in two days' time.' Silence. He leaned in to give me a kiss. I obliged. But just before reaching my lips, he pulled back. Instead, he leaned in towards my ear and softly whispered, 'Don't forget to leave the address on the fridge so I can check you're safe.' I nodded.

Just two hours later, there came a thunderous knock on her front door. My friend hadn't said she was expecting anyone or any deliveries, so I jumped up to open the door. There he was. With a bag. His bag. 'Thought I'd stay too, in case you get lonely.'

'Well, I'm not really allowed to have my boyfriend stay over. I promised it would only be me,' I said.

'Is that so,' he said, dumping his bag on the green velvet sofa. 'What she doesn't know won't hurt her. Anyway, I'm hungry. What you cooking?'

'I'm not,' I said and got up to exit the room.

The next moment, I felt a hard push from behind. My body slammed into a pearl painted wall, my head nearly missing a gilded frame-encased painting depicting green forest trees. I knew this man was a narcissist and emotionally and verbally abusive, but he had never touched me before. He had threatened but never actually crossed the line. Of course, he had crossed many lines from the outset, but I refused to accept that. Until now.

I turned 'round and found him breathing heavily over me. 'You make me so fucking mad,' he said, fist raised. I looked him straight in the eye, the cogs in my brain whirring. I was used to the broken glasses and plates and yelling by this point. That was common—my fucked-up normal. This was not. 'Fuck you,' I screeched. 'GET THE FUCKKKK OUTTTT!' I could feel my face roasting with rage.

His brow furrowed as he lowered his hand. I could tell in that moment he realised what he'd done. 'I'm sorry, I'm sorry. I'll leave. See you day after tomorrow,' he said, slowly moving away.

I watched as he exited, and I collapsed into a heap on the Persian carpet, unsure whether to bawl or laugh. The adrenaline still pumping, I gathered my thoughts. *What the fuck are you doing with this arsehole? He doesn't pay a damn bill, nor does he buy food. He doesn't even have sex on the regular.*

I looked deeply at the forest trees with the big stumps and gnarly roots detailed in the painting and decided there and then to ground myself in strength and exit the relationship. In those days, we didn't have cell phones, so I couldn't text breakup or ghost him. Plus, I had my clothes and furniture, and it was my apartment. Fuck, fuck, fuck!

I took several sharp breaths and steadied myself with a final *fuck you* breath. I could do what I needed to do. I could go gather my things and leave. And that was exactly what I did with the help of a couple of friends.

Because I had extended so much of myself to this man—trying to heal him, bandage his broken bits—I was neglecting myself. I needed to heal parts within me, and Spirit knew the only way to crack me open was to let my heart feel the most immense fear. In the silence of the apartment that day, after he left, I could finally tap into a portion of my own darkness and lack of self-worth.

I was lost. Plain and simple. But I was never alone. The old patterns of wanting to fix everything and feeling worthless were still present and would rear their head again later in my life. But for now, I could breathe.

CHAPTER 3

Mother and Father Complexes

#waybackwhen

'The game of life is a game of boomerangs.'

Florence Scovel Shinn

Mamma and Dadda influenced me at a subconscious level, and their mark showed up in the patterns I exhibited throughout my relationships. First, there was Mamma's over-giving, her bid to sustain relationships. This was certainly a trait I succumbed to. Then there was Dadda's dominance, his effort to maintain control for fear of abandonment. I, too, displayed this dominance. So I moved into adulthood with a fear of being abandoned by those I loved while constantly trying to fix them and control situations, my ego refusing to accept that I was but a speck of dust certainly not in control of anything in the vast universe of life.

As I waded through my history and photos while writing this book, I began to see just how much my parents' stories became part of my story. I developed mother and father complexes that would reside within me throughout life. Only now am I beginning to untangle these complexes and separate who I am from my social conditioning. So join me as I go back and remember.

Dadda and Mamma on their wedding day

MARTYR MAMMA

I was raised by a nurturer. My mother. Mamma, as I called her. She is strong and determined, yet quiet and poised. Mamma fixes things and people, constantly adapting to make circumstances better. How she feels inside is irrelevant, but how she presents things to the world is vital. A tiresome facade but the only one she knows.

Mamma was born in Johannesburg in 1936. A definitive year for the blueprints of racism becoming law via the Representation of Natives Act (1936) and the Native Trust and Land Act of that same year. All rights to land and voting were permanently stripped away from Black people during that year. Mamma would have to wait a half century to cast her first vote in the country's first all-race democratic elections in 1994. She was born in the Malay Camp and grew up in Marshall Street in central Johannesburg. It's here where John Vorster Square was later built and became the infamous site of countless interrogations of anti-Apartheid activists and where several brutal murders were committed—the most well known being that of South African Communist Party activist Ahmed Timol, who died in October 1971, and that of political detainee Clayton Siswe Sithole, a mere twelve days before the release of Nelson Mandela in 1990.

Malay Camp, or Fietas as it was commonly known, had a Rainbow Nation spanning Chinese to Black to Indian and everything in between. Its demographic was as varied as its more famous counterparts, District Six in Cape Town or Sophiatown in Johannesburg. Raised by a single mother, Mamma was different. She looked different with her slanted hazel green eyes and long straight brown hair. Her name given by a local Chinese shopkeeper was Maylahn.

Mamma was classified as Coloured since she was mixed. Her father was either Japanese or Chinese; she never knew. In fact,

Mamma never knew her biological dad and despises her mother for not sharing any details of him. All she had was a single black-and-white photograph of a handsome Asian man in a greyish Western suit and tie—with an English version of his name. All she heard was that he was known for running gambling dens. A single photograph capturing who she is, who she lost, who she will never know. It was a part of her life she could never fix.

When you try to trace an Asian familial connection, an English name is useless, and this was all she had. His name when he landed on the shores of southern Africa was Henry bloody Ford, after the American car manufacturer. My heart aches for her.

My lost grandfather

THE IDENTITY TRAP

Mamma and Dadda were married in 1959, the same year Buddy Holly, Richie Valens, and the Big Bopper died in a horrific plane crash. Not a great omen by all measures. By this time, Mamma had already been a survivor after being forced out of her house in her twenties. She fleetingly mentions how her mother chose her stepfather over her. A wound that remains septic for her, a hurt that remains even after her mother's death.

By the time I was born, my mother's identity was wrapped in that of my father. I learnt this way of being from her—stemming from a desire to be kept safe and protected. In reality, it is a faux belief that the alpha male can save us or give us our value. Mamma forgot her own Goddess power, as would I. She showed me just enough of her inner strength for me to learn to armour myself. But she could not give me enough knowledge of battle, and I would end up using the shield too often to keep fighting for dying relationships when I should have used the sword and cut myself free.

The pursuit of happiness seemed like war to me as I tried to figure out why it was always a battle between love on one side and hopeless fear on the other. I never seemed to win the raging fight inside me between these two feelings. My love for others always stemmed from my fear of being unloved.

Mamma's sense of identity had always been under attack. She would tell me stories of how Dadda defended her honour against his own domineering mother. Her mother-in-law was cruel with an exaggerated sense of grandeur because her surname was

Golding. Her self-importance hinged on their finances, and their ability to fund and own a church smack bang in a whites-only neighbourhood added to her status in her small fishbowl of a community. The church was likely built to preserve the land from being confiscated during the Group Areas Act, but it ended up being another way to diminish my mother's worth in comparison.

Mamma fondly recalled, 'Your father always stood up against that old goat. He never allowed his mother to belittle me or my children.' Dadda got some other things right, too. He kept his promise to build Mamma a home and secured a plot of land where our family's house was built—far away from his own siblings and parents. Mamma always clucked about it. 'We showed her. She nearly passed out when she saw we had our own home,' she would say, smirking. But over time, Mamma's self-worth was weaved entirely into possessions and her home. Her perceived status compensated for hurt and loss and the pain.

Mamma proudly entertaining in her own home

In truth, my parents were bound together by an insatiable codependency. Their partnership, presented to the world as a united front, protected their honour. Their authenticity, well hidden. Their fear of abandonment, kept secret. They danced out of sync, except when united against a common enemy.

He was sociable, and she, a loner. His jovial mood was encouraged by copious amounts of Brandy, sneakily stashed in the broom cupboard. I remember how she always smacked his hands away with the swipe of a dishcloth, discouraging his amorous advances. She grew more and more tired of him as the years passed by.

I remember being about six years old, heading off after church for the obligatory visit to Dadda's mother's home. She was bed-bound and too ill to attend service in her lauded church. Despite her poor disposition, she would yell from her bed: 'Frank [my grandad], go get the pot. Stop being so stupid.' All the while, we stood sombre at her bedside. Dadda, Mamma, and I. Dadda saw it as his duty to visit every Sunday after church.

So we stood silently while a few words were exchanged—the obligatory greetings amidst the smell of imminent death, mothballs, and cheap musky perfume. No wonder Dadda was so domineering; he feared being bullied like his father was and being stuck in his childhood trauma. Unfortunately, Dadda never recognised Mamma's kindness or worth. He had his own demons, being cast aside by his mother in favour of his brother. And so my Mamma nurtured this man who needed to be fixed because of his dysfunctional upbringing. Meanwhile, she placed her own trauma on the back burner, resenting him as the years passed.

By Christmas of 1979, Mamma had had enough of the bullying, so off we went—she and I—to the Company Gardens in central Cape Town. Every Christmas I got to choose any dress I wanted, and that was my end-of-year gift. This year, I was excited to wear my spanking-new outfit, a pale blue-and-white dress, on the train ride with Mamma. This was my first time on a train, as we headed to Company Gardens. A day outing like this was usually unheard of, and I spent the day feeding fish, pigeons, and squirrels with Table Mountain as a magnificent backdrop. The cable car to the top of the mountain was a pipe dream I would only realise when I had my firstborn child. Money was tight when I was growing up, and boarding a train into the centre of the city was a luxury in itself.

As Mamma and I sat silently in the sun, I looked at her. At forty years old, she was trapped. 'I was going to leave him, but then I found out I was pregnant with you,' she confided as she emptied the last of the peanuts from the bag. 'He wanted another boy. You were supposed to be his namesake.' I fed the squirrels with the last peanuts and listened in silence as she released her pain. I was sorry that I was born, and she was tied down to the responsibility of it all.

The parent dynamic between them was traditional in every way. Mamma did the cooking and cleaning, and Dadda was the breadwinner. Dadda was set in his ways, and Mamma was subservient. Of course, packaging the dynamic as 'traditional' only makes it feel less harmful. Traditional is such a cop-out, a way to ease the discomfort of what was a very imbalanced marriage. The truth was that there was a domineering figure who did not lift a finger in the home. He didn't change a single nappy or even wipe my snotty nose. Surprisingly, he did wipe my bottom until the age of six. I would yell jubilantly, 'I'm finished,' and Dadda would excuse himself to do what needed doing. Four wipes. Aside from this, Dadda contributed financially and so felt that he did his fair share, providing neither emotional support nor assistance on the domestic front.

When I was born a *laat lammetjie*, nine years after my sister and eleven years after my brother, Mamma and Dadda were already in a toxic relationship. It seems odd to say that they were neither happy nor unhappy as a couple. They could sit and bond over radio dramas and enjoyed watching wrestling together on the telly. Saturday afternoons, I would see them both yelling at the television set, particularly animated as wrestlers bounced around in the ring, doing slams and clinches.

They always ate lunch together, although Mamma prepared the lunch and cleared and tidied after. They were an imbalanced duo who needed each other. Like two halves, clinging to each other to make a whole. Mamma always referred to Dadda as a 'good provider,' nothing more and nothing less. I don't remember him ever complimenting her, yet he was acutely aware of her atten-tion-grabbing beauty. His jealousy was evident when he abruptly exited social gatherings.

They celebrated their silver anniversary—twenty-five years together—when I was in my teens. She never left. He never left. They came close to divorce when I was eighteen years old. There were more and more verbal confrontations with the odd physical altercation, but Mamma, although petite, could hold her ground. He never beat her, nor she, him, but I witnessed them shove each other, yelling obscenities. Perhaps this is why I became comfortable with the odd shove and push by boyfriends.

I wished they would just bloody divorce back then. Probably exactly how my children must've felt watching me bicker in both marriages propelled by my own pain, my own fears, and my own codependency. But in my childhood, divorce was not commonplace. When I was in high school, only three friends had single mums, but the rest were in stereotypical two-parent families. No biracial couples. No same-sex parents. Looking back now, it's bizarre that that was the norm. And if there were couples from different racial backgrounds or from the LGBTQ+ community, it was kept on the down-low.

Even though Mamma had such a miserable experience in her marriage, she still subconsciously communicated to me that the union itself—not necessarily the happiness thereof—was important. I remember when I married my first husband, who I'll call David, Mamma was in a foul mood because I didn't plan to wear a veil. I wasn't a virgin after all, but she was losing her shit over it. I wasn't about to say, 'Oh, by the way, I have a bun in the oven.' I felt guilty and ashamed of being three months pregnant, worried I would embarrass my family, particularly her.

I had learnt to attach so much importance to what others would think about my mother, although I didn't care what people actually thought of me. I knew she saw me as an extension of her, and so, here I was worrying about what the community would think and how embarrassed my family would be. I concealed what should have been an openly celebrated upcoming birth, knowing the shame Mamma would have felt. After all, she threatened to not attend the wedding if I didn't wear a bit of tulle stuck to my head. I ultimately succumbed to the veil, not the truth. Ironic, as all my friends knew and were rejoicing, quietly of course. The anger and resentment were all over me as she stared me down, twirling the veil in her fingertips. 'Aren't veils for virgins?' I asked, not able to resist a bit of passive aggressiveness. I learnt from the best.

Tantalising tulle

What was important to Mamma was that I was having a full-blown wedding—what had been denied to her. She and my father completed their nuptials in a registry office—no family members present. My mother was made mute by years of being unseen, and she couldn't help but practise an icy resentment, effectively freezing me out if I dared to resist. No doubt, I've been guilty of this exact behaviour at times. Whereas these days, I can take ownership for my projected pain onto others, Mamma, well, she is stuck in age-old patterns.

Young Mamma

HONOURING HER

Today, Mamma continues to be silently strong, but decades have taken their toll on her petite frame. A few weeks prior to the pandemic, I noticed her struggling with her eyesight, and she had a minor procedure to remove cataracts that had been affecting her vision for the last few years. True to form, she never told anyone. And no one cared to notice.

I've witnessed that she is physically slower but keeps as busy as if she was forty-four, not eighty-four. She is resigned to having no opinion and observing in pained silence the shenanigans of her offspring. I sit with her on her sofa in an effort to recharge our relationship. Her eyes wander around the room, and she brushes back her neatly cut grey hair. She is lonely and has a firm shield of protection around her, keeping her feelings to herself. Her favourite memories are of travelling to destinations that were simple and stark. She once travelled to Mumbai with friends. She recalls how people were poor, yet happy. It's as if she is trapped in this gilded cage of her own making while sharing stories of people whose lives she wished she lived.

What if she could have been happy sleeping on the floor and washing from buckets? What has the double-storey home with a salt pool and a security guard actually given her? The absurdness of it all is not lost on me. Home for me will forever be the first one I knew—the single-storey home on the Cape Flats, and I suspect she wishes she could go back to those simpler times, too. Now she is stuck in the grandiose home my older brother placed her in. Where she lives now is a large leap from her former lodgings, as Cape Town's Atlantic Seaboard signifies the upper echelons of the societal matrix.

Still, she rejects any claims that she feels imprisoned and declares, 'What's the point of complaining?' I cannot be upset for she has sacrificed much, namely her happiness. Nothing could be sadder. But I can tell she is not as peaceful as she used to be when she and Dadda lauded over their simple home in Annadale Road in Athlone, a street off Thornton Road, the very road where children were murdered in the Trojan Horse Massacre. At least there, she was the queen of her own castle.

I remember that childhood home well. Dadda would ardently tend to his orange and yellow marigolds. Being house proud was vital, and rankings hinged on your front garden presentation. Dadda was never a great gardener and was especially unskilled with roses, unlike the opposite neighbour who boasted spectacular roses of varying colours and heights. Of course, roses and dahlias are for those who excel at having green fingers.

In my community, the men in the neighbourhood proudly displayed their floral skills however they could. Even though Dadda was a dire gardener, he was a smooth talker. He could sell ice to an Eskimo. Instead of considering his gardening endeavours as dismal failures, Dadda used to trumpet marigolds as the rose of Athlone. His hardy marigolds bloomed in all shapes and sizes—a sea of orange and yellow bulbous heads swaying in the breeze in our front garden. 'Marigolds are majestic,' he often quipped, adding that anyone could grow roses. Yeah right, Dadda. I used to be a captive audience to his knowledge of flowers and often thought the marigolds were far lovelier than the thorny rose bushes.

I often consider how my parents' love story was akin to the dependable marigold rather than the rapturous rose. A dependable union sans romance. Because Mamma never knew her father, the abandonment was ever present. She recalls she was born from a brief fling. The story goes that he wanted them to return to China with him, or maybe to Japan during the Sino-Japanese

War. Her mother refused or perhaps was too scared to leave. Each time my mother tells the story, I hear the deep-rooted resentment in her voice at the weakness of her own mother's inability to keep the family together. Unlike her, she stood the test of time and endured with my father.

I, on the other hand, gave up. More accurately, I chose to walk away. Yes, that's right, I learnt to step away from the patterns my mother had shown me and instead chose ME. And if I had to do it over again, I would choose ME again and again and again. To Mamma, this was selfish of me.

Mamma proved that she could secure a husband and ensure that a father remained steadfast in our lives, giving absolute sanctity to the vows of marriage. I once wrote her a letter acknowledging her sacrifice for our perceived stability. Her sacrifice has not gone unnoticed, not by me anyway. I don't dismiss the strength it took for her to stay by his side till the very end. But the sacrifices she made were at the expense of her happiness. Had she tried to pursue her nursing dream, we would have all been perfectly okay being raised by our single mum, but the stigma and fear of such immense change kept her stuck.

Still, for all the ways I wish Mamma's life played out differently, I honour her. She was generous in so many ways. I remember how she would squirrel away some Rands and cents to purchase at least one gift for me at Christmas. My older sister always gave her money month end, and Mamma would hold on to that money without telling Dadda. She was attentive to what I desired as a teenager and gifted me my first tape recorder, a silver one. It was a very generous gift for Christmas, and I suspect she saved many months for it, taking a little bit here and there from the grocery budget. This gift was topped only by a pink camera the following year. Of course, Dadda took credit, too, but I knew it was her.

She always tried to give me what she surely never received as a young girl. We never had a Christmas tree, except one year when my sister made the effort, but even then, it was merely a decoration alongside the tinsel streamed against the walls and crepe paper bells in green and red adorning the doors. But Christmas was never about gifts; it was about the food. Tons and tons of yummy treats like peanuts and raisins and peppermint crisp fridge cake, trifle, chicken, lamb, and loads and loads of roast potatoes. And, of course, this was all prepared by Mamma.

A young Dadda

DOMINEERING DADDA

As I stare at him now on a grim sunny day, he looks hard. Stony-faced and harsh. Still, silent, stiff. The stereotypical tough-guy brawny exterior. He's not wearing a hat today. He never will again. It's odd. He always wears a hat. His brown fedora or trilby strategically placed on his head during spring and summer. Autumn and winter welcome the tan or brown flat caps echoing the tawny leaves. His dark green and red Kilmarnock stark against bare tree branches. My knuckles clench tightly 'round the hard rimmed edges of the coffin, mindfully feeling the smooth wood, eyeing the glisten of the over polished bed in which Dadda is resting.

It's nearly the end of winter in the southern hemisphere. The air is devoid of birds chirping. It's stifling. Sweat clings to every part of my body, seeping strangely through the armpits of my sombre dress. I'm nervous. He's wearing his favourite white tuxedo jacket. The maroon handkerchief cheekily peeking out his pocket. He looks suave. His ensemble strangely unbefitting for the sombre occasion.

I swing back and forth to the tune ringing in my head. I close my eyes and feel the vibration of lyrics—echoing through my limbs, settling painfully on my heart. The lyrics of 'Run' by Snow Patrol and sung by Leona Lewis as I write this chapter. I recall details of that painful day.

My toes squish together uneasily in my patent leather kitten heels, both feet tapping nervously.

I jerk back to reality as a smartly dressed woman taps me on the shoulder, edging me along. She's wearing a hat, a pillbox hat. My gaze remains on him as my mind wanders to his shoes. Those shoes are definitely spit-polished to an inch of their life. That's simply Dadda. Always smartly presented. A doctor of chiropody. I feel slightly stronger, emotionally ready. Suddenly feeling a surge of confidence in my own ensemble. Presentation is vital to him.

His words reel repeatedly, relentlessly in my brain. 'Always remember to look your best. People judge on first impressions. Especially when you Black. How we look tells them who we are. When our faces are shiny and clean, when our shoes throw back our reflection, when our clothes are neat. That tells them we have pride. We decide who and what we are. They do not.'

Childhood memories flood in. I remember Mamma combing my hair, pulling it neatly but firmly back and plaiting it adorned with powder-blue ribbons. Nivea or Vaseline dabbed on my face. My school socks, a gleaming white. School shirt starched. Dadda insisted I polish my shoes. In fact, teachers did notice. They would comment how even old shoes can look brand spanking new with a bit of shoe polish. Shiny shoes, clean handkerchiefs, bright ribbons. I am grateful for the arsenal of grooming tips I've accumulated across several decades.

I pull my mind sharply back to the present as I glimpse the sharp edges of the timber, the shine of the chrome and the brilliant white satin. Satin is such an odd choice. I lean closer towards him, drinking in his sallow face, his brows, his mouth. It frankly still does not look like George, no matter how hard I stare, following the outline of his jaw, his forehead, his bald head.

His head reminds me of a hard-boiled egg before the shell is removed. Boiled eggs were staples in our fridge when growing up. Mamma said they made for a quick, easy snack. The shell is smooth and cold, yet quite odd. You know it's an egg, but something is off. Well, that's how it feels now as I gaze at him. I know it's him, but something is, well, just not quite the same. I see him now tending to his marigolds, the yellow and orange bulbs. I remember how he once hustled his way to become the caretaker at the French Embassy in Newlands, Cape Town. Money was tight and the family home needed to be rented. Housing for caretakers was free. The embassy's perfectly coiffed rose garden, on display for dignitaries, was about to be swiftly converted to swatches of orange and yellow bulbous heads.

'Oh, far more fetching and eye-catching,' he would casually remark to the Ambassador, with persuasive charm and confidence. 'The rose,' he mischievously added, 'is not even the national flower of France. Is there not a saying along the lines of an English rose?' This struck a chord with the Ambassador, and within months, the French gardens had quickly changed hue.

As I still stand gazing at his lifeless body, I recall his gall. A wry smile twitches on my lips. I have no wretched cries like Mamma. No detached blank stare like my brother, and no sighs of resignation like my sister. Simply a sad smile and memories.

Here I am at twenty-five years old, a newspaper columnist with two daughters, a husband, and no father. I moved cities to be near Dadda. The irony of it all. My youngest daughter is only three months old, and Dadda didn't get to meet her. The only child proudly born in Johannesburg, in a free South Africa. The doctor cut short all joy by announcing an emergency surgery to remove a portion of her intestines. After forty-eight hours and with her still not feeding, the white hospital walls closed in. I was consumed with making promises of attending church if God just saved my newborn baby from having surgery. The Universe granted me my wish. I, however, never kept my word about the church malarkey as I never enjoyed attending service. Little did I know that in another city, a mere two-hour flight away, Dadda was gravely ill.

By the time I finally reached the ICU ward where he was, I was unaware of his drastic weight loss, and I buckled seeing a huddled comatose frail body. The strong father I knew and loved, now small and helpless. 'Oh, Dadda, stay with me,' I said. 'Oh, Dadda, you gotta see your granddaughters. I moved. I actually did it. I came home. I can see you every day now.'

His limp hand enveloped mine, and I saw his long thumbnail, clearly in need of cutting. As I grabbed some nail scissors, the nurses entered, bluntly announcing it was time for his bed bath. The indignity of it all. I left to have a smoke outside, several in fact, as I poured my heart out to a hospital porter also puffing clouds of nothingness into the morning sky. 'Please visit him,' I said between sniffs, puffs, and whimpers. 'He loves a bit of gossip.'

Mamma never mentioned how ill he was. Neither did my siblings. He always wanted to lose some belly fat, but his weight loss was shocking. Nothing like when he previously embarked on cycling a few years prior. A sight to behold—a rotund man in his sixties balancing precariously on a racing bike, holding tightly onto the bent over handlebars. Surprisingly, he was still fairly athletic and agile, managing to cycle a good twenty-five kilometres on a good day. He would find a local hawker selling vegetables or fruit, standard in South Africa, and secure himself a seat (the hawker left standing) and a free newspaper to catch a break and people-watch. He loved to people-watch and to gossip with anyone who fancied it.

I have a lot of his character, keen to mingle with people and hear their story, but only when I'm in the mood. He could be grouchy as well, once leaving a Christmas lunch early simply because he found my brother's girlfriend's family 'blerrie irritating,' as he put it. Perhaps it was simply because they were white. He rarely could hold a poker face, feelings laid bare for all to see.

I carry the same up-and-down, in-and-out way of being with me. What you see is what you get. I'm a bit of 'a circus,' as Mamma puts it. Always flitting from one country and continent to the next. Running from something, towards nothing, but never knowing why. Revelling in the freedom of it all. 'Starting afresh invigorates me' would be my standard reply. Finally, I found myself in the same country as my parents, and my Dadda bloody dies on me. What a fucking cruel turn of events. Two years earlier, he was healthy, able to travel, and had a zest for life. What about the promise he was going to live longer than his own dad, who clocked out at ninety? For fuck's sake, Dadda, you bloody fucked it all up.

Dadda was admitted to hospital the very day the removal van arrived to collect my boxes in Johannesburg. Cape Town within sight. A new beginning. Packers in their blue overalls cheerfully loading my firstborn toddler's worn slide and bits and bobs of baby paraphernalia. Plastic toys, paint pots, a furry donkey, a seesaw, and a black tricycle. The crockery and cutlery haphazardly wrapped in newspaper sheets, heralding my byline. And I had no idea.

I am numb and confused at the funeral. How did it all go so wrong? I feel the nausea of uncertainty, gurgling like gargoyles in the pit of my stomach. The grotesque heads breathing life into the loss and copious thoughts of *now what?* Mingled with *fuck, fuckity fuck, fuck* swirling in my brain. George Hermanus Francois, my father. Strong and reliable, and now gone. Just a few weeks before Princess Diana's death in August of 1997. Three years after the first democratic all-race elections in South Africa. At least he got to cast his vote.

MEMORIES

Lyrics always seem to answer questions deep in my soul. Feelings of grief, pain, and growth are regurgitated, released, and reborn through song. As 'Run' now repeats on iTunes, I remember.

I remember how he flew to England with Mamma to meet his third grandchild, my firstborn. It was three months after her birth when my folks boarded the flight to England, saddled with my favourite South African condiments—Mrs. Ball's Chutney, frozen koeksisters, and samosas. It was the nineties, and you could travel with anything in your luggage, short of a live chicken. They packed their spanking-new suitcases to the brim with bricks of butter and biltong.

When they arrived, I remember how Dadda rolled on the floor in our one-bedroom East Croydon flat, holding my little baby girl high in the air. He was delighted. Proud. Now he had bragging rights and could inform his two sisters who lived in England that he was there too. His sisters emigrated in the sixties and went abroad via ship. In those days, travelling by ship was far more affordable than flying. Calling them up from our apartment in East Croydon and telling them he was in England was simply a 'Fuck you' from him to them. Gosh, the animosity he felt towards his siblings was deep, and the feelings were mutual. They didn't bother to attend his funeral. His younger brother did—he was a priest—he had to. The one sister he did adore and love deeply had died years earlier, the only sibling he enjoyed a strong bond with.

Dadda was always treated as less than in his own family. The youngest son, he was a rebel and never really played by the rules. Choosing to marry a woman from a different city. They didn't approve of nor accept her. He showed he didn't care by choosing to build a home himself after being stonewalled by his family from securing a property. Despite having two kids at the time, relatives refused to give him first bid on a family plot. His rebellious nature saw him purchase a plot of land far from them—a decisive move. Then he built out our family home, which was a twenty-minute drive from the enclave of the other siblings who lived along the same road or within a block of one another.

I remember Dadda's laugh as raucous, engulfing that one-bedroom flat that my first husband and I rented on his meagre salary. Dadda's voice would escalate the more whiskey he drank.

Loud decibels synced with high-pitch jocularity, like an ill-rehearsed vocalist. He was often hiding insecurities and likely depression, too.

But here in the flat, Dadda laid flat on his back, holding his granddaughter high in the air, stocky fingers firmly grasping her chubby tummy. He made gurgling sounds to make baby react, his forehead wrinkling as he tried all sorts of ridiculous faces to elicit a reaction. His protruding belly didn't hinder him in the slightest as he rolled this way and that, chuckling. 'You Are My Sunshine' blared from Capital Radio. I knew they disliked silence, so I obliged by keeping the radio on throughout the day.

But this scene of joy was not the norm. Dadda was neither a great husband to Mamma nor an exemplary father. However, he was reliable and always had your back. Always. Ready for a verbal fight or physical altercation, whichever response resolved matters. If I asked, he delivered, if he could. No strings attached. No reminder of what he risked. I was always grateful and often told him so. I miss him.

To Mother, he was 'a great provider.' In fact, when he died, she inherited a mortgage-free three-bedroom house with a small lump sum stashed in the bank. He always wanted her to be independent and not reliant on their children. 'Children can turn on you. They get too big for their boots,' he would say. She relied on him financially all her life, and he liked that. Now that he died, the house was all hers. She was the madam of the manor. His parting gift for being a shit, belligerent husband, I suppose.

Though he was a provider, he was also extremely frugal. When I was a kid, he would send me over to the neighbours to get their broadsheets after midday every Sunday. The timing was crucial, as he calculated that the morning newspapers would have been perused by them in the morning hours and then discarded by the time the clock struck twelve. This is when I would be despatched to collect said discarded newspaper with all the inserts. The neighbours, aware of his cunning, would smile and oblige.

Dadda was never afraid to do what he wanted and say what he wanted. When he met my first husband at Johannesburg International Airport a day before our wedding, he shook his hand firmly, welcomed him to the family, and expressed how thrilled he was that I was no longer his responsibility.

As we drove to my wedding, the antique rose-coloured bulbous dress with luminous layers of tulle swallowed us up. We sat silent, swatches of satin wedged between us. As we clambered out, we enjoyed a naughty smoke together, the first time I lit up in front of him. The Peter Stuyvesant cigarette smoke wafted in the air, tobacco mingling with the lavender and rose scents outside the quaint stone church. I'm not a practising Christian, but somehow we ended up here.

I was wearing the bloody veil my mother insisted on, perturbed. But Dadda's hand steadied mine. He was getting ready to walk me down the aisle, and I was chuffed. He was smiling too, seeming genuinely happy for me. We faltered for a split second, prematurely wanting to walk. 'Must go slow, pace, pace, and pace,' he muttered to himself. 'Ta-da-da-daaah, ta-da-da-daaah.' Sweat trickled down the back of his neck and he grabbed his handkerchief, gave a swift wipe, and grabbed my hand again. Off we went. 'Here Comes the Bride' in time and in tune. He never did make the wedding speech, though. My brother thought he'd had too much alcohol, and he had. But he still sat there as proud as punch, as if he had paid for it all, whiskey glass aloft in toast.

Wedding march

He was a proud man battling many of his own demons. A mixed-race man being raised in an era when colour dictated your fate. Against all odds, he achieved so much. As a young man, he found himself in the spotlight. A newspaper clip announced, 'George, the young man who claims to be the first non-white auctioneer in the entire country at only twenty-five years old.' The South African broadsheet depicted his portrait. Heralding the achievement of a Coloured man during the sixties in Apartheid South Africa was unusual. To grace the pages of a local newspaper with a large accompanying photo, a tremendous triumph. His dark hair frames his gentle face as he stares at me now from the yellow framed clipping hanging in my hallway.

WHAT LEADS US HERE?

What made my father who he was? As I consider his background, I remember how much we are all impacted by the context in which we are raised. For my father, that was with one older brother and five sisters. He is one of the youngest—a stocky lad who broke rules and was never favoured by his mother. In fact, she only briefly raised him when the British Empire still ruled the Cape Colony, but he was sent off to another province to be looked after by an aunt at a young age. He never spoke much of this, only mentioning it in passing, but it no doubt had an impact on who he became.

His parents were Frank and Caroline. Frank was a twin, and the brothers ended up marrying two sisters. Dadda's parents were blessed with many children, while his uncle and aunt had none. George was closer to his uncle than his own father, whom he regarded as weak, controlled by his mother. He vowed from a young age to never be weak; instead, he became a harsh bully.

Ironically, the narrative of his own life was more closely aligned to that of his mum. A big woman with a sharp tongue, always in her darkened room, with features akin to the not-so-delicate Queen Victoria. How apt that she adored Queen Victoria. My father's dad was a cheerful but spindly small man who whiled his days away chewing tobacco with his spittoon always nearby.

When Dadda did stay with his parents, it was in an imposing house in Albert Road, Lansdowne, where I would later play as a little girl with my cousin. The dark red cemented verandah always gleamed with the faint smell of polish, and the musty-smelling house held its grandfather clock and brass knick knacks.

I still remember the grand stained-glass front door and the formal sitting room no one was ever allowed in. The room boasted glass showcases hosting even more knickknacks, ranging from porcelain dolls to china bells and bizarre glass thimbles. To the left of the creaky hallway with its maroon Persian patterned rug was Ma Golding's room. Straight ahead was the combined dining room and informal area with all walls covered in old portraits of distant family members of Jewish heritage. Golding was originally Goülding, and the story goes that they were Jewish Germans who fled Nazi-occupied Poland. The African side of the family was less clear. My father once said that we were part Xhosa and then years later, added the San people to the mix. Details were sadly missing—a result of some family members who, perhaps, were not keen to accentuate our African heritage, but I shall never know.

My father was always fond of names and saw his own name as a symbol of elitism. In a world where he held no clout because of his race, he consoled himself with names that he believed elevated his status. Both my siblings have two or more names, and I obediently followed the tradition, giving my son, George the Second, a total of four names. Who needs four names but there you go, embedded nonsensical doctrines live on.

Dadda honestly believed that he had bestowed Mamma with the most priceless of gifts—a name and a legacy of belonging. A surname which he believed would elevate her and alleviate the burden of not having known nor inherited her father's surname. She was a bastard, and he could save her. Sadly, he also constantly reminded her that he had given her a name, emotionally pummelling her into submission that she should be eternally grateful.

Her wish that she would be a merry widow when he kicked the bucket did not seem to ring true as his wooden coffin disappeared behind the red velvet curtains ringing in his final farewell. As the furnace flared, his favourite hymn, 'Up from the Grave He Arose,' belted out from the congregation, 'With a mighty triumph o'er His foes.'

I still miss him. I know he would have a lot to say about my two daughters and two sons—their behaviour, their attitudes, and their lives. He always had a lot to say. As with my mamma, I am sad that he continued certain patterns throughout his life, but I also honour him and his generosity. He always had a sandwich at the ready for the hungry, a shoulder to cry on, made time to listen to people and cheer them up with his wise words. He was the only protector I knew.

In many ways, I wish I knew more of him, more of his story. Thankfully, I do remember his most prudent advice—his two key lessons for anyone learning to drive. I choose to apply the advice to life in general.

Dadda: 'Keep your eyes on the road ahead, don't worry about what's behind you or to the side of you.'

Me: 'Er, okay, Dadda, but what if I want to overtake?'

Dadda: 'Just stay in your lane. There's no rush.'

The second was this:

'If your petrol gauge is on E, do not ever panic. E is for *Enough*, not *Empty*. You still got enough to get you where you wanna go. Keep going, and if you're going downhill, drop the gear stick into neutral and cruise. Once the road is flat, level up.'

CHAPTER 4

Siblings' Subconscious Influence

#fam

'Love yourself enough to learn to love others without losing yourself.'

UNKNOWN

BOETA

INTERACTIONS WITH MY TWO OLDER SIBLINGS INFLUENCED me from a very young age. A brother I called Boeta and an older sister, I called Sis. Our relationships would impact how I'd interact and relate with others throughout my adult years. I found that I succumbed to any fragment of a relationship they

93

offered me because I was scared of 'losing' their love or approval. Compounded by my ability to perform in front of guests as my parents lauded over me, I also nurtured an unhealthy relationship with both siblings from a tender age and could not differentiate between what was a loving relationship and what was transactional. Any relationship where I was acknowledged was good enough for me, as it made me feel valued, seen, and worthy.

Boeta was always very generous and gave me my first travel adventure at the tender age of eight. He had paid for my air ticket. It was the early eighties. I boarded a plane from Cape Town to Johannesburg. A mixed-race girl from the Cape Flats on her first adventure and *nogal* on a plane. My stomach churned, my hands trembled with excitement. I held tightly onto the emblazoned fat cat hand luggage Mamma gave me. The bag was a dirty orange colour with an enormous stripy yellow-and-black cat painted on it. 'Easier for *them* to spot you,' said Mamma reassuringly. I bloody hated cats.

Them being Auntie and Uncle. They would collect me at the airport. Boeta was way too busy to taxi me to my lodgings. It would take me years to discern between a transactional relationship and one from the heart space. Although financially generous, emotionally, he was stingy. As a young girl, I internalised our relationship deeply. Despite it being devoid of emotional connection, I never stopped attempting to strengthen emotional ties—a habit I carried well into adulthood with emotionally unavailable men.

Boeta was ambitious and was earnestly creating a trade union from scratch, preparing for the imminent unbanning of the

African National Congress. A mineworkers' union would be a defining moment against the Apartheid Nationalist government and the fat cats of mining. I'm to be in Jo'burg for a week, spending an entire day with him. The air hostess in her navy blue suit with ostentatiously titled headgear grabs my hand. She puts a little board around my neck. 'Minor,' it says. She smiles. 'You stay close to me, my dear,' she says, leading the way up the stairs into the belly of the aircraft. My eyes are like saucers as I look at the rows of seats. 12 A. 'Here you are, my dear, right at a window,' she says, settling me in and placing my cat bag in the overhead locker. 'If you need me, simply press this button,' she says pointing to a cream button with an orange image. Nodding at me reassuringly, she leaves, pushing past the streaming passengers as they impatiently shove their way along the very narrow corridor.

How odd that these inexplicably narrow corridors are foisted on air passengers of all races, and all sizes, and all ages to jostle and juggle luggage and sit together in the air. Diversity and integration in mid-air, yet enforced segregation on land. Everyone settles down, the pilot speaks amidst static through the intercom, the pretty air hostess with the ruby lips demonstrates how to click the seat belt minutes prior to take-off. The engine roars, the exhilarating speed pushes me back in my seat. I look out the window and giggle as the buildings become smaller and smaller like little Lego pieces. The Boeing 747 tilts up, climbing higher and higher above the clouds. I feel free and on top of the world.

I was going to see Boeta. Several days passed before I hear from him. He is visiting tomorrow.

I put on my sunflower-yellow pinafore. It has ornate white lace etched across the neck and puffed sleeves. Uncle frantically looks at the clock on the brown tiled kitchen wall. Auntie, Uncle, and my cousins are invited for lunch at their friends' home, which is an hour away. 'We have to go now, Jackie, but you can wait in the yard,' stammers Uncle. Boeta is running late as usual. He hasn't bothered to call. Everyone accepts this behaviour without question. He has successfully managed a repertoire, perfected across many years, to make us feel special by simply gracing us with his presence, always shrouded in impatience, yet received with gratitude by a multitude of relatives.

Boeta wasn't born with this superior air of confidence. In fact, he was often overlooked at school—in the shadows with his acne complexion and low self-esteem, dismissed by his female teenage peers. An accident on the Klipfontein Road in Athlone smashed his dreams of being a football star like his hero Pele, and he delved into a sole mission of making a name for himself. These days, though, he is nothing of his former high school self. He is confident, doggedly committed to spearheading a unionist labour voice—a first in a country besieged with uncertainty. Short in stature with a thick wad of dark brown hair, a dazzling smile, and sparkling brown eyes, he is self-assured with a bizarre gigolo gait around women. He is my absolute hero and can do no wrong in my childlike view, and admittedly, this perception lasted well into my adult years.

I beam at Uncle who towers over me. 'Okie dokie, sure, Boeta won't be too long,' I say in my happy, sing-song voice. Their cream Ford Cortina reverses out of the dusty yard. I wave, both hands in the air. I sit on the concrete step just outside the back-door. A smile firmly plastered on my shiny, Vaseline face. When Boeta comes down the road, I shall easily spot him from my vantage point. I stand up. I hop on one leg. I do a little jig. I must think of something smart to say. Perhaps mention Darwin. Or the book he gifted me: Trotsky's *Iron Heel*. An alarmingly odd choice for a little girl, not even ten. I will think of something. Nothing is more important than getting a reassuring tap on the top of my head.

I rummage in my plastic bag for my favourite Chappies bubble-gum. I find it. Under the crumpled tissue and the rubber bangles. I boast an impressive bubblegum stash. I casually flip my long plaits and kick a pebble with my brown leather sandal. It collides in the red dust creating a small mini cloud—dust particles settling on my stubby toes, now mucky from digging into the red gravel to bide the time. I peer at my watch with the cracked face and stagnant dial. I wave at passersby in their Sunday best heading to church. The men tilt their fedoras while the women wave with gloved hands, complimenting my *mooi* white anglaise socks pulled up over my knees.

If you happy and you know it, clap your hands. Clap clap. My tiny palms smash together in tune and in time as I sing. My care-free voice high-pitched behind the waist-high wire gates. Most houses in Eldorado Park have wire gates. In fact, it seems they are standard for Coloured townships. They certainly are popu-lar at home on the Cape Flats, too. Gates facilitate neighbourly gossip yet proudly demarcate property. Respected homeowners whose gates you have to open, usually with a squeak, to enter. I skip around the yard. I drink water from the outside tap. I hear a distant bell chime. The same family with the lady in her smart fuchsia hat and white gloves wave once again. Her brow furrowed as she tries to peer into the yard. Was church over already? My fleeting panicked thought is *That was quick. Where was Boeta?* I wondered.

Church lasts an average of two hours if you consider tea and biscuits following a sermon. I rub my gurgling stomach. I'm hungry. The stinging in my eyes feels pricklier. It must be the dust. The Ford Cortina pulls up. 'Wow, Jackie, you got home before us?' asks Auntie quizzically. I steady myself. In a desperate attempt at light-heartedness and deflection, I quip, 'I didn't go. Hallelujah, you're home! He must've been busy. May I have some custard now, please?' My well-rehearsed sentences spilling out feverishly, a tad incoherently. Inside my head, I chant, *Tears, tears go away, come again another day.* I blow a bubble. It splats on my face.

Boeta eventually turns up a few days later and takes me to a mineworkers' gathering. 'Amandla!' I shout with my fist in a Black power salute. 'Awetu!' comes the miners' thunderous unison reply. I feel special. Special enough to forcefully erase the hurt, the feelings of being unseen as I take in the power of his presence, desperate to please him, to fix whatever I need in order to be seen, to be acknowledged by this man who I adore. Boeta is the dominant male in my life, aside from my dad.

Unfortunately for me, I had also placed my brother on a pedestal, spinning an illusion around him of what he is and what he means to me. I see now that the relationship I forged with him lacked any boundaries and that was my own doing. Boundaries that I subsequently failed to have in place with all relationships going forward. The relationship, as I've evolved into a more discerning adult, has nowhere to go. We remain estranged now.

I understand now that we all have our own journeys and one is not more painful than the other, for they are merely varied perspectives of life. Because of my relationship with my Boeta, I got accustomed to fighting for attention through achievements and then accepting the limited time he did spend with me with gratitude. This was all I knew. Because of his desire to be the patriarch and our acceptance of it, it moulded me into what I authentically was not—a submissive female, happy with bread crumbs of attention as it was way better than none at all.

All I knew was to cater to his needs within his schedule, very similar to how Mamma behaved, and my sole purpose was to please the men in my life. Mamma did it so well—stoically and without complaint. It's not his fault nor is it hers. It was my own deep-rooted childlike need that saw me measure my worth against the acceptance of others.

Even as an adult, I wanted him to see me, acknowledge how hard I tried to do the right thing, witness how hard I fought, how hard I loved, how strong I was, how loyal I was, to reassure me that I was worthy of love and that I was, indeed, loved. I was turning into what I disliked the most in others: maternal martyrdom. *Breathe*, I say. *Breathe*.

SIS

Complicated. That about sums up my relationship with my sister. Nine years older than me, I do have fond memories of her being protective of me in my younger years. The middle child, she left school early and easily slotted into working life. Self-reliant and independent, she had a hard exterior and soft centre. Fondest memories of her were her regular phone calls home and her annual visits throughout most of my teenage years, where she was laden with small gifts for me. When I was younger, she used to piggyback me to bed, and I missed her terribly when she moved out of the house in her twenties. She was a dutiful daughter in many ways, always giving monies to both Mamma and Dadda. But tensions between her and Dadda were always at an all-time high. He never approved of her choice of men. She felt robbed of any male figure protecting her throughout her life. This resulted in grief and sadness, which saw her and me, to a lesser degree, become armoured with emotional walls built as fortresses around our heart space.

All she sought was happiness, but then again, true happiness eluded her as it did me, simply because our cups of self-love were dry to the fucking bone. I recognise the pain and unkindness of life having taken its toll on her and isolation is how she currently chooses to traverse through life. I found through my healing that the acceptance of all my pain as lessons and the release of said pain as progression in life only occurred because I accepted the duality of my existence. As I observe her, I learnt that blaming others for my pain will only rob me of living a full and happy life. A life of hope would be denied if I held on to what coulda, woulda, shoulda happened five, ten, or even twenty-five years ago. The past is done. The now is all I have. Tomorrow is not guaranteed.

Releasing was key for me. Sometimes I would partially release and continue to begrudge all those people I claimed did me wrong. This was only stifling my own flow towards abundance. I had to truly let shit go if I sought to live authentically and in the present moment. PRESENT. It's a gift. We cannot change the past; from it we can only learn and grow and in the now, the present—we can live mindfully, trying to make conscious decisions, because today's choices will become yesterday's memory and simultaneously determine tomorrow's flow.

I have hurt my sister quite a bit. I can be a queen of swords with my words, and she can retaliate as venomously as she gets. But one memory, above all, stands out: the day her pain and hurt overtook her so much that she threatened to beat me to a pulp with a hammer. I was in my early twenties, and being me, my fury and indignation overtook any fear I may have had. As the adrenalin pumped and soared through me, I declared, 'Go on,' then, 'What are you waiting for?' I felt defiant and betrayed, immune to her hurt as well. In fact, I was downright nasty and unforgiving. So was she in her vitriolic anger.

All she ever wanted was not to be judged, to be accepted. The irony is that I wanted that, too. Where she chose to rebel and isolate herself, I chose a different route. I became a people-pleaser, desperately trying to be a good daughter, or heeding to the standards of Boeta and trying to impress future partners.

Eventually, I was forced to pause on this trajectory by the Universe, which you will read about in the coming chapters. I was forced to *breathe*. Forced to accept all of me and vow to love myself, flaws and all. I learnt to forge stronger boundaries as I battled alone through hurtful challenges later in my adult life. I can be self-absorbed, my confidence verging on arrogance, but that was because I thought her a bitch, and she me—yet, we yearned for love and closeness. The irony is that neither was able to achieve even an iota of that closeness because of self-loathing. Nothing to share other than unkind words and incessant jabs. We mirrored our parents' behaviour yo-yoing between the control and dominance of Dadda on one extreme and the self-pity and martyrdom of Mamma on the other. We re-enacted our role models rather than assuming our own identities.

I couldn't fix our relationship. It has moments of closeness but is peppered more with distance and misunderstanding. I'm acutely aware that this ancestral pattern needs to be broken. She does not talk to my mum, and my middle daughter doesn't talk to me for now. Both scenes steeped in hurt. The cycle perpetuating a lineage of pain. For now, all I can do is heal me. Eventually, the healing within will flow outward as I walk in faith and gratitude.

I am grateful to my siblings for lessons which I only grasped decades later. I can now self-soothe the little girl who felt abandoned and didn't have the tools to comprehend and heal her own lack of self-love. There are only two people I need to fully love and make proud. They are not external relations but are within me. The first is my wounded child self and the other is my aged self for as I grow older I need to feel and know joy and, hopefully, look back at my life lived with a sense of peace and gratitude.

Love is complicated between family. If only I had the tools of leaning into my breath at a young age, to tap into my heart space and fill up the void I felt with self-love. Now I know. Now I grow.

CHAPTER 5

∞

Becoming the Saviour

#loveisblind

'Being attached to someone is not about the other person. It is about your own sense of inadequacy.'

SADHGURU

LITTLE DID I KNOW HOW EARLY PATTERNS IN MY LIFE WOULD play on repeat through my relationships. I would carry particular ways of being into my adulthood, without ever fully seeing what I was doing. Most notably, I had learnt the skill of being a saviour. The dynamic I hated between Mamma and Dadda—she playing fixer and he playing the one needing fixing—would show up time and time again in my life. And it would take me more than one relationship, or marriage, to wake up and practise a new way of being.

FAST ROUTE TO MARRIAGE

That new way of being was not going to occur in my early twenties, for sure. Yet again, here I was, single and somewhat carefree. My career as a reporter was flourishing and I was happy. Even more so when I met David.

A fellow work colleague had slept with him months prior. A drunken one-night stand was how she put it, adding that he worked on a rival newspaper. The same one I had just serendipitously applied for as a general news reporter. Her one-night stand would become my first husband.

I'd be wife number two for David. Story of my life, always the second, never quite managing first place and never asking the right questions as to why it never worked out the first time for them. Oh, who wants to complicate matters with facts. I was way too busy glorifying a temporary status quo. Happily convincing myself that second meant success. Surely, the secret lies in second chances. Always better the second time round, eh? I could add many more of these little gems ever ready up my sleeve to assure my ego that this one is, indeed, a worthy winner for matrimony. I was always the quintessential believer that lemons equal lemonade.

David initially worked on a financial broadsheet, and I worked for an investigative tabloid (not the stereotypical British tabloid but an esteemed publication that was independent in its views and constantly challenged the Nationalist Apartheid regime). Both were considered among the best newspapers in the entire country. Mine edged his in reputation, and he would eventually jump ship to join my post a few years later. For now, we were pursuing our separate careers until we would eventually meet.

I was spending my final days as the youngest in the tabloid newsroom, having celebrated my twenty-first birthday in a dingy jazz club in Johannesburg's trendiest suburb called Hillbrow, where jazz band Loading Zone played and renowned jazz guitarist, Jimmy Dludlu, cut his teeth and wowed my colleagues. My Dadda made an epic Brandy infused speech and handed me the obligatory twenty-one key, which is a community rite of passage. The key signifies your ability to open doors and make choices as you embark officially into adulting. The wooden key was special as it was carved by Mamma's half-brother.

Dadda handing me my 21st celebratory carved wooden key

I was climbing the proverbial career ladder and finally one year on, I collided into his world on the financial broadsheet.

At this point, I had just broken up with my abusive ex who resorted to stalking me, incessantly turning up at my new place of work. I didn't want to end up like Mamma, financially dependent on anyone. Yet, despite earning a living wage before securing a post on David's broadsheet, I had still ended up in an abusive relationship. I found solace in chasing career promotions and pay hikes. I foolishly believed this would enable me to exit future relationships more quickly because I had the financial means to up and leave when I wanted. When I first secured this brand new reporter position, I happily sauntered into the newsroom, brimming with confidence and oozing *I'm dat bitch* vibe. At this point, I was so chuffed with myself and my new job that there was no way I would've connected the dots that money was neither the ticket to freedom nor peace. Self-love was. My higher self would later awaken, embarrassed at how low my bar really was being set.

Still, the job did provide a real boost. Before landing the position, I was barely able to put fuel in my blue Volkswagen *Voksie,* and now I could level up. I had 'made it' and felt euphoric about it all. My pinnacle of success at this stage of my 3D life.

My first day on the job, and there he was. Precisely described by my colleague. Sitting upright, light brown hair slightly spikey with a furrowed brow, he happily tap-tappity-tapped on his keyboard using a two-finger technique. That's the ability to type on a keyboard using the forefinger on each hand to knock out paragraph after paragraph of newsworthy copy. God only knows how he could write, edit, and be a successful journalist, sub-editor, and news editor with that technique, but there you go. Miracles never cease.

Today, despite being in his fifties, David still has not mastered the art of the ten-finger type. Back then, I found his awkward method pretty cute. When I first set eyes on him, he was wearing a double-breasted suit and tie (it was that type of establishment). He peered up with his large doe-like green eyes and smiled. He was actually damn handsome, and at twenty-two years old, I thought I was the hottest shit in stilettos. He would be the one punching way above his weight. The minute I saw him, I thought, *This fucker, I'm going to marry him*. His British accent and sardonic humour only fuelled my fantasies. He was a bit of a lad about town, having shagged at least three reporters I knew of, one of which still worked in a senior position at the financial broadsheet where I was now the rookie. Still, I was not deterred. My sights were set, and he seemed enamoured with me too. My ego was fully engaged to what she wants, she gets.

My fondest memories are of the times I was on night shift at the broadsheet. He would stay late and wait for me to finish, after having completed his own day shift. Very sweet indeed. It never occurred to me that it may have been just a matter of convenience, since I would then drive us home. But such is love, an ability to just drink the Kool-Aid you choose. I would beam, my rose-tinted glasses firmly fixed. I was already planning the wedding in my head.

Mind you, I was not the type to even consider marriage, but there I was thinking it would be the shizzle to get married. *His handsome, intelligent ass works hard, and our babies would be gorgeous. Why the fuck not?* All other suitors fell to the wayside. To be fair, none of them had reliable jobs, but did fit my bad boy type perfectly. He was the furthest thing from a thug, and I thought, *Why not try something different?*

A KINDA PROPOSAL

Before long, we had moved in together. He was four years older than I and already had a son back in the Midlands, England. As a typical Libran, the wedding was planned in my head as we sipped coffee in the newsroom, cigarettes burning in overflowing ashtrays alongside our desktop computers. Something deep inside of me said I needed to earn his love and attention…that something deep inside of me was actually my Ego feeding my unworthiness and fear of simply being me. Although confident that I was attractive enough, I was fearful of losing love and being unworthy of being loved forever. Bam. Just like that, I over-gave without hesitation. Draped in fear of possible abandonment, I launched forth, determined to work at this love. I needed and wanted to impress. After all, I had just left an abusive ex and David was surely going to be my protector.

One day, out of the blue, he presented me with a lovely dainty diamond ring in a box. I was expecting earrings of some sort, but as I opened it, I gasped. 'Oh my God, an engagement ring!' I jumped up and down in excitement, hugging him tightly. The images of Hollywood movies permeated my brain. I had been proposed to before, several times in fact, but never had an actual ring been presented on the spot. And here was one presented in a bloody actual box with the flip-up lid. *OMG, OMG, OMG.*

I looked across at him oblivious to his deer-in-headlights expression, which I would get to know in the coming years. He shifted from side to side, gave an awkward clearing of the throat, looked at me, and said, 'If you want it to be.' I erased the nonchalant response with my extremely active imagination. I clasped down with both hands and ran to the alter in my head. I can laugh at it now. Bless him. The poor fella could hardly say, 'No, it's not an engagement ring, you silly cow.' He couldn't dash my dreamy declaration to smithereens. So he opted for the easy option of, 'Yeah, okay, sure.' After all, I would be his second wife—clearly not the love of his life. She got a bloody huge sapphire, apparently. But I was a good substitute. Besotted, eager to please, a fantastic cook, a keen lover, and above all, reliable and loyal. For his first wife, he had written a song to show his adoration in the first year. I got a surprise bunch of flowers stuffed in the fridge six months after our first daughter was born and we were together for nearly two years already. Nevermind, I was thrilled. A love ballad was never my thing anyway. Too clichéd.

Time passed this way in our marriage. The wedding came and went. Then we had our daughter. All along, in true Queen of Cups mode, I was empathic and self-sacrificing, so *he* felt loved and safe. I never insisted on reciprocity, and it was a good thing I didn't. Sure, he occasionally brought me strawberry Nesquik in bed pre-kids and made us brekkie on the Saturdays he took off work post-kids, but I felt the burden of trying to be both a good mother to the children—taking them to the park and library, having friends over as they grew older—and also being a good traditional wife—cooking meals daily and trying to have the house just so. He tended to choose to work most weekends as the years clocked on and checked out emotionally.

Still, I honed my arsenal of ingratiating stunts. Something deep inside me needed to earn and keep his attention. He gave me plenty of attention when he felt like it, but when he didn't, I was left feeling abandoned. One particular night, early in our courtship, comes to mind. We were supposed to head out for a night on the town with some close friends. He was taking a longer than usual bath, and I tentatively entered. The time: 7:45 p.m. Drinks were booked for 8:00 p.m.

'What's up? We gonna be late.'

There he was, sitting in the bath, eyes closed. Total darkness.

'I'm not going. Don't feel like it. Want to be alone. Switch off the light, goddammit.'

That thingy deep inside of me welled up. A combination of exaggerated childhood memories of being shunned to second position, coupled with a nurturing concern for his well-being. I never went out in the end, stripping off my glad rags for a comfy pair of PJs and a night of silence. Utter silence. My ego was bruised, my unworthiness fed, and my fear of simply just being me, the woman who would normally go out and have some fun with her friends, crushed. Pleasing him to prevent rejection propelled me forward throughout the relationship. The marriage was wrapped in fear, as I pledged to work harder at this love. Trying to heal his wounds, forgetting about my own.

David was from a divorced family. My folks were still together, having already celebrated their silver anniversary. Despite many crises, they remained married. His father had abandoned his relationship with him in favour of a stepson. His mother had moved on to marry a narcissist, and having to use dishwashing liquid rather than shampoo peppered his childhood memories of her second nuptials. She has since married for a third time to someone he approves of.

He needed me, and I wanted to be his saviour. I needed the love, and I did whatever I thought would make up for his abandonment issues to get it. I don't remember him ever asking me about my childhood or my pain. Truth was, my parents had no happy union, and my childhood was potentially as painful and dysfunctional as his. But how easily we can shift our perspective to the laments of others and so avoid focussing on our own shit.

My arsenal of people-pleasing attributes included over-giving and over-nurturing. I found a way to make sure that all the men in my life were taken care of even if they didn't take care of me in the manner I desired. As the years rolled by, my self-sacrifices got larger and larger. The more I overextended and betrayed myself, the more I hoped against hope that my life would improve. That those I had given so much to would finally rain an abundance of gratitude, love, and nurturing over me. Of course, it would never happen. Oprah once said, extracting a pearl of wisdom from Dr. Maya Angelou, something along the lines of that we should never expect others to treat us as we treat them; as "you're setting yourself up for a life of disappointment. Allow people to be who they are and then decide if you want to continue nurturing a relationship or not." The choice is always ours to make.

UNREQUITED LOVE

On David's thirtieth birthday, I tried to entice his parents to have a joint birthday dinner with us. He had mentioned years prior how he had longed for them to have a meal together. My idea was shot down by his father who clearly still could not bear the sight of his mother. His mother, however, was keen, wanting her moment to shine since she had married up on her third go. Neither ultimately conceded to the idea. This made the fix-it urge within me a thousand times more potent. After thirteen years together, here we were in the same pattern. He knew none of my wounds, and I wanted to fix all of his.

But it was never either of our responsibilities to fix each other. That journey into self has to be done solo. It's a journey through hopelessness and grief that erupts eventually into self-love and acceptance. Fortunately for me, I recently broke one ancestral pattern by having David stay and spend time with two of our three adult children, with me being the gracious host, at peace that the grown-up children could see an amicable relationship existing between me and their father despite nearly two decades of divorce.

Back in the nineties, when his birthday came around, he didn't even have time to rub the sleep from his eyes before I was hovering over him, precariously balancing a ginormous chocolate cake. Happy Birthday carefully etched in white buttercream boasting the obligatory flaming candles—all thirty, no less. He propped himself up, as the look of shock softened to tenderness. As he blew out the candles, I urged him to make a wish. I'd always wanted someone to surprise me with a huge birthday cake. I'd always wanted someone to encourage me to wish and believe in miracles. He smiled, blew the candles out, then turned over and went back to sleep.

'Oh, he's so exhausted, shame. Sleep, Honeybun.' I returned to the kitchen, cut myself a huge slice, poured a cup of coffee, and lit a cigarette. The plumes of smoke wafted in the air, dissipating to naught.

A few years later, it's *my* big thirtieth. I have our latest addition, a four-month-old son. There is so much to celebrate. I'm so excited as I wake up. The girls run in wishing me a happy birthday, and I bounce my baby son on my knee as I open the birthday card. 'Oh, Gemsquashy, oh, Bellybops, that's so sweet. Mummy needs nothing; her pressie is your little brother, George, our Zozo.' I get them ready for school, and David is already out the door of our semi in a quaint cul-de-sac in SW20, heading for central London. The day passes by as usual with household chores, children ferried to and from school, a quick cuppa with a friend, and finally carting my daughters to gymnastics and swimming, all with bubsie in tow.

My kindly neighbour has set up a birthday celebration for me, and we head over at 6:30 p.m. The plan was set so that David could join us. The kids are excited, having rabbited on incessantly about it that morning. It's a bit of a late tea for the little ones, but it's a special day. It's not every day Mamma turns the big 3-0. Crisps and birthday cake sit on the table in the neighbour's light-filled conservatory. The wall clock shows 6:30 p.m. Tick. Tock. Tick. Tock. 7:00 p.m. Still no sign of David.

The children are restless and hungry. I call his mobile. No answer. Tick, tock. Tick, tock. 7:30 p.m. Tick, tock. Tick, tock. The clock strikes 8:30 p.m. It's their bedtime. My baby needs another feed and nappy change. I relent and let them each enjoy a sausage roll and whatever they want including a teensy slice of cake. The unlit candles squished to the other end of the cake to preserve a happy birthday jingle. We make a final call but still nothing. Finally, I usher my three out the door. It's time to acknowledge defeat and leave.

The girls hold hands, not forgetting to each take their slices of birthday cake carefully wrapped in pretty napkins as we head 300 metres home. I thank my neighbour for all her efforts and make some lame excuse as to David's no-show. We approach the house, and it's dark. Pitch dark. Could he have been delayed at work, I wonder?

We make a bit of a ruckus as you do, trying to get two kids ages five and seven through a front door while holding a baby, leftover party food, and the obligatory balloons. I trip over his shoes in the hallway as I go to turn on the lights, tell the kids it's far too late to bathe, and get them cosily into their PJs. I do the 'sign of the cross wash' myself, which is face, bits, and under the arms, then tuck them into bed, read them a story, and change the baby once more.

I eventually muster the courage to peer into our bedroom. There he lay, fast asleep. Tears silently roll down my cheeks. I swallow hard. My heart splinters. I breathe deeply into the comforting smells of my baby boy's neck and whisper, 'It's going to be okay. You're going to be okay.' Nothing left to do but get the baby settled and go to bed. Tomorrow is another school day, after all. I try to blow off my pain. Perhaps he just had a busy day. But even my tried-and-tested method of changing the narrative fails me.

Why was I so hurt? This was not the first time I had felt wounded in our years together. I knew he despised the commute to work and reminded me daily. It was his mantra. 'I hate schlepping into London. I hate it. I'm tired.' What could I do? Clearly, it was me who was the burden, but I understood to a degree. The financial responsibility was on his shoulders, while I had desperately tried to further my career attending a film course at the London School of Film while seven months pregnant; childcare costs in England were sky high and to pay for three children would be exorbitant for a young couple. Furthermore, I had no grandparents nearby to help out except a friend's mum who was a surrogate granny to the children.

When we left South Africa to have our first baby in England, it wasn't easy. I was twenty-three. This wasn't my first time in the United Kingdom, but it was my first time pregnant. Previously, I had attended the Thomson Foundation journalism course attached to Cardiff University. Back then, I was still single and carefree. This time, things were way different. I was married and with child. We initially stayed at his friend's in Streatham. She gave up her room for us, we paid a discounted rent, and I helped her paint her front room. Learning to balance on a ladder in my third trimester whilst wielding a roller wasn't an easy feat. To make matters worse, I had never painted anything in my life, not even my nails. I had no friends, no family, and no one to talk to day in and day out. I could not stand it beyond six weeks, and I eventually took the initiative and secured a dank basement apartment in Thornton Heath. It fitted in our meagre budget, and it was across from a park, which lifted my mood. Not for long, though.

Soon after moving in, we returned from an arduous coach journey to his family in the Midlands to find our house ransacked. We later found out it was the caretaker's son. He had trashed the place. I'd never been burgled in South Africa, but here in England, I got a firsthand taste of crime. The matchboxes I had carefully wrapped to look like gifts on the Christmas tree were scattered across the floor. There was no money to purchase store decorations, and it had taken me days to get all the decorations just right for my first Christmas in Blighty.

Exhausted, I looked at the mess. I cried. He consoled me. The window was broken. The microwave minus the inside glass plate was stolen. I tracked it down at the local pawn shop and was cursed at by the shop owner. So I tried the police, who simply said their hands were tied, so I was ultimately left to walk home with my enormous belly in the rain. The green dungarees, a Camden Market purchase, dripped green dye all over the road. My tears mingled with the rain as it started to pour. The very next weekend, David was off on a work trip.

David: 'Essential.'

Me: 'I'm scared to be alone.'

David: 'Nothing I can do. The trip to Scotland is a must.'

Two weeks later while packing his suit away, I found rugby tickets in the inside pocket. As a former journalist, I knew the difference between an essential story and a freebie jaunt.

I would discover a pattern in our relationship. I would sacrifice in any way I could, and he would do as little as he could. At nearly nine months pregnant with our first child, I felt so alone. I trekked to prenatal check-ups on my own, fainted in a supermarket, and went to bed hungry on at least one occasion. I remember that last event vividly. He had come home with a takeaway of a chicken leg and thigh, which would be our dinner. Unfortunately, his friend had tagged along and proceeded to eat my portion of the meal. We couldn't afford to feed him, but he didn't know that. I was starving, but then I didn't want David to think I didn't want him to have his mate around. With a growling tummy, I went to bed early while they laughed and regaled stories of their younger selves.

BEING MOTHER, BEING WIFE, BEING CAREER WOMAN

Fast forward to us returning to South Africa, our firstborn now a toddler. By this point, I'd secured a diploma from the London

School of Film; coupled with a journalism background, this would be a great fit, and in a city that I knew and loved—Johannesburg. We briefly live in an apartment and our return means I can work as well, which will see us improve our accommodation to a rented detached home. Things seem better now. Perhaps we can make this work.

Then one night, he goes out. 'I'll just lock you in. Shan't be long,' he says.

'No problem,' I yell back, knowing we have only one set of keys. No need to distrust his reassurance that he shan't be long.

After a few hours, it's getting dark, so I phone a mutual friend. 'Do you know where David is perhaps?' I ask. 'I'm worried.' I can hear the music in the background and loads of voices.

'Oh, he's here,' she says. 'I'll call him.'

Anger of proportions I would only experience once more in my life well up inside of me. I'm shaking now and can't manage to press the line receiver to my ear. I yell so loudly that our young daughter wakes up. 'What the fuccccckkkkk? It's been nearly four fuckkkinnnngggg hours, you arse fucking hole. What if there was a fire? We're several floors up.' I'm delirious. I throw the phone receiver with such force against the floor that it cracks. I cry and curse and then curse some more.

'The acid test in any relationship is whether the good times outweigh the bad,' he used to always quip. Well, the definitive result of the test was more than clear.

STILL CLINGING ON

My career was flourishing but family life was floundering. I consoled myself that other people I knew were equally challenged in their relationships and vowed, yet again, to make this work in my overcompensating manner. Then I became pregnant with my second daughter and worked till the day I gave birth.

I was a media editor at the time and thoroughly enjoyed my career. One day, I returned home from work, and something didn't feel quite right. I put it down to another exhausting day of deadlines. I was nine months pregnant and opted to work within seven days of my due date in order to secure more time off once the baby arrived. After feeling a sharp pang, I knew I needed to go to the hospital. I screeched that our toddler needed to be taken to my brother as I prepared to drive to the hospital. But soon, the agony doubled, and I knew it was not feasible for me to go behind the wheel.

An alternative plan is hatched. David has to drive me to the hospital. Not happening. My brother's girlfriend at the time is summoned to both drive and take care of our eldest daughter. Mayhem ensues with me reassuring my toddler that I'm not dying (amid her frowns of concern), remembering my birthing bag, and David behaving like a lost fart in a perfume factory.

Hours later I was induced, and our second daughter was born. But there was a problem. Meconium was in my waters and once she was born, she wouldn't feed. A paediatric specialist informed me that a portion of her intestines had to be removed and an emergency operation was scheduled. I remember sitting in the waiting room having a smoke. Yes, you could still smoke in waiting rooms back then. The sun shone through the hospital window, and I looked up and vowed to go to church if only God saved my daughter from having to go through an operation. Spirit obliged.

Miraculously, the nurse came in and said all she needed was a shit. Yep, her intestines were clogged, and after she had a poop, all was good. I cried tears of joy but promptly forgot my promise to the Universe. I never attended church and never said thanks in the coming days. Well, the Universe balances everything all in good time. Although I had given birth a second time to a healthy baby, my own rebirth towards a healthy self would take many years still.

That was 1997, a memorable year on many fronts. My dad passed away three months later and never got to see my daughter, who is the same star sign as he was. A feisty yet sensitive Taurus with the strong horns of a bull and a fiery temperament. She was the smallest of my babies, weighing only 3.025 kg. A healthy weight but tiny compared to her older sister and itty-bitty compared to her brothers, who would be born four and fourteen years later. The grief of my father's passing overwhelmed me, and I often found myself clutching my baby girl, imbuing her with my sadness and loss rather than feeling my joy at her light.

Of all my babies, she is the one I feel most guilty about because I was not my strongest emotionally in her earliest years. She was also the one I had to leave to bring our belongings from one city to the next. Again, it was me driving thirteen hours straight from Johannesburg to Cape Town with my red Uno packed to the brim, including zebra finches (two sweet birds in their pink cage—acceptable then to us, certainly not now).

I think I also suffered from undiagnosed postpartum depression, which made the grief of losing a parent even more devastating. David tried to console me, but I never truly felt his emotional support. In fact, he'd often go out rather than stay in with me. I couldn't blame him. I was a wreck. He even went out to drink at a bar with work colleagues while I was at my parents' home attending a prayer meeting for my Dadda's passing. The truth of this would emerge years later.

I believe Dadda missed out on something special with my daughter. To make matters worse, there was very little male bonding happening for my daughter. During the many telephone calls I made to the ICU to check in on my father, my husband was not around. When I called weeping that my father had had a heart attack, he did not rush home to comfort me but stayed at work, returning hours later to find me numb with grief, playing blankly with a toddler and breastfeeding a three-month-old baby. I had asked the Universe for a hardworking husband, which I got, but I forgot to ask for one who was emotionally available as well.

The no-show or the last-minute show was a pattern. I remember laying in Croydon's Mayday Hospital in March 1995 with the most amazing maternity staff, the most kind-hearted midwife, and a perfect baby girl—our first daughter. As visitors came and went to congratulate the new mums, I lay with my baby swaddled with not a card or balloon in sight. David, true to form, was late. Visiting hours would soon be over.

I lay there cuddling close to this amazing little human and immersed myself in the moment. She was a Pisces cusp Aries baby, born March 20. A sensitive soul with a kind disposition. I felt sad that he was not there alongside me, but I was determined to nurture this indigo child. The other visitors glanced at me sadly, likely assuming I was a single mother, unloved and unsupported. They were partially right. I felt unsupported and alone. Eventually, he arrived with nothing else other than my requested strawberries and cream Häagen-Dazs mini tub of ice cream. Within ten minutes, visiting hours were finished, and he left. Ten whole minutes of nothingness.

A few years later, I suffered a miscarriage. We were in Johannesburg, forging out our careers. I was pregnant again a mere eighteen months after my second daughter's birth. Four months into the pregnancy, I miscarried unexpectedly. Blood everywhere. I wrapped myself in towels and frantically called him at work. 'I'm coming,' he said. An hour passed, and he still hadn't arrived. I grabbed the car keys and got someone to watch my daughters. I sped to the hospital. By this time, the towel was blood-soaked. I staggered into the lift, and on arrival at the doctor's suite, I was swept into A & E for an emergency procedure. I lay there under the blinding white light, seeing the blurry outline of his face. My cheeks, stinging from the salty tears. I had nothing to say.

A year later, we returned to Addiscombe in England. Another move, another fresh start. When it came time for the girls to start school, we got family help and secured a semi-detached family home with a huge garden backing onto playing fields. At the time, I still believed the tiredness and responsibility David felt having to work to provide for us and pay the mortgage was the reason our marriage was struggling and why I had to work even harder on the domestic front to make sure I was a good wife.

When I sat alone in the garden of our semi-detached house in West Wimbledon, pregnant with my third child, as he chose to work another weekend back to back, I convinced myself that he was sacrificing to provide for his family. He just needed another holiday, and all would be well. An adventure together to quell our wanderlust would do the trick. For now, at most, all I would do was complain about his absence. I didn't understand that one cannot change another; one can only change one's self. I refused to accept the reality that was blatantly revealed to me from the very start. I was still adept at performing, especially for those I loved. It was an ability I had honed since childhood, and it wasn't going anywhere fast.

We spent four years here with our two daughters before I was expecting a son. This boy would not wait. A sharp stab in the side of my belly, days before my expected due date, and the taxi had to be called. I couldn't possibly drive. I calmly got into the cab, talking enthusiastically to the cab driver so he would at least think I was due for a routine checkup and quickly head to Kingston hospital.

Ten minutes into the ride, I could not hold it any longer. I screeched out in agony. 'The bloody baby is coming!' The rest is a blur except for the part where hospital staff said, 'Sorry, Mummy, it's too late for an epidural.' *Fuccckkkkk*! No pain relief. I was convinced I was going to die in childbirth. I'm dramatic like that. With a slew of nurses and training nurses and doctors, one politely asked, 'They're in training. Do you mind if they witness the delivery of your baby?'

'Whatttt? I don't bloody care. Get this baby out. Jesuzzzzzz, it's hurting.'

'Okay, hun, breathe. Just breathe.'

'I'm sorry for cursing. Fucccckkk! Sorry. Fucccckkk! Sorry.'

I delivered the bugger on all fours sans pain relief, and he weighed an astonishing 4.2 kg. I called the kids, who were with my mother (she had come to visit), and told them they had a baby brother. That Monday, two days later, I was taking the kids to school again. Back to the same old routine, mulling the same old unanswered questions in my head. Why was my overgiving not fixing matters? The answer was surely in taking a trip circling the globe. A change of scenery would do the trick; that was my optimistic take on my dismal marital circumstance.

Baby 1   *Baby 2*

Baby 3

SEARCHING FOR SOLACE

After ten years together, I still tried to put up a fight to save us. We took the plunge and traversed the globe in the hopes of resuscitating our dying marriage. I hoped that feeding our need for adventure could kickstart what I believed we once had. I was most excited about Fiji, after perusing pages upon pages of brochures of pristine white beaches and coral waters. Then we arrived. I saw he had booked a backpackers' lodge, where the beers were at the ready but not the beds. It certainly was not child-friendly. And definitely not romantic. Instead, we'd be staying in hostel accommodations with drunk youngsters wanting to surf and scuba dive. Breakfast was basic hangover food: a single slice of toast with black coffee. At least I befriended the staff and got extra toast and lashings of jam for the kids.

The first morning there, David was already gone before breakfast. He had booked a boat ride out to sea to enjoy a spot of scuba diving. His favourite pastime. While he was out, I found us more suitable accommodations with clean linens on the beds and nice fresh white tiled floors. The new place even had a water slide for the girls. I also secured a tour guide to drive me and my eight-, six-, and two-year-old around town. There was no way in hell I would be at my dream destination only to have someone fuck up my experience, not even if that someone was my self-absorbed baby daddy.

I explored the beautiful sites Fiji had to offer with the children and driver, a kind and patient Indian man with jet-black hair. He explained how he had left Kenya with his family for island living. He was like a rent-a-hubby. He swam with us, answered all our questions, took us to purchase food, and provided me with much-needed adult company. We even went to Natadola beach with him. It is one of the most beautiful beaches in the world, and my girls still remember it to this day.

Through travelling, I've learnt that the world is filled with beautiful generous people who offer immense kindness and laughs when all seems lost. I will be forever grateful for the time this man bestowed on us when only just the night before I was crying, altogether considering abandoning the trip because of loneliness. He will always be etched in my memory as the kindest human who continued to accompany me and the children as we trekked across the width and breadth of the island. David and I were clearly on different pages, traversing the island separately. On the third day of exploring on my own with the children and said tour guide, I spotted a wonderful resort along the black sand beaches and snapped up a bure for the final few days as a victorious fuck-you-too to shitty marriages, scuba diving, and hostel accommodation. This wooden five-star lodging was set in tropical parkland with lush palm and local banana trees paving the way to its front door. Idyllic postcard-perfect Fiji had arrived.

It was obvious the globe-trotting did nothing to mend the marriage but rather further highlighted the gaping holes. Instead of searching inward and seeing why I was so unhappy, so alone, and so hurt, I was still looking outward at him. I was drowning in despair but desperate to cling on. I was good at that. For thirteen years, I could talk myself out of anything while the Universe shook its head in disbelief.

As I reflect, I think, *Crikey, Jax, take a breath. Breathe. Take stock and stop running from the truth.* But I refused to face my reality. I just couldn't see it then.

When we explored the exquisite island of New Zealand, it was I who drove from North to South Island, stopping along the way at recreational parks for the kids. David refused to drive, ever. Before kids, after kids, or at any time during our marriage. Not even when I was in labour or miscarrying. Not when his mother was in critical condition. And certainly not for a scenic family drive. He did, indeed, have a driving licence, but he felt claustrophobic in the car. Somehow, he could happily sit in the passenger seat for hours on end with no side effects. The more kids I had, the more ferrying I needed to do. From extramurals to playdates, then grocery shopping, or lugging kids' friends as the proverbial mum taxi.

Again, the pattern played out. I did all I could while he sat passively. Mamma's age-old adage of husbands being 'good providers' kept repeatedly reverberating in my head as I hopelessly applied this to David—a breadcrumb of consolation for lack of love from an emotionally detached partner. I was waiting for the love from him, while my soul was waiting for the love from me.

When we were with the children, I saw David as fun-loving whereas I was the disciplinarian. He was the weekend warrior dad who played with them, while I made them eat their veggies. My Mamma was the disciplinarian, too, but it was different from Dadda. Sure, he provided financially, but he never played with us. *Children should be seen and not heard* was the motto he seemed to live by. When he did stop for a moment to spend time with me—I noticed. I still remember how he sometimes found and placed a chameleon on my hand, spending five minutes to see if it would change colour before tending to his plants.

I want my children to be happy, and I'm grateful for the world travels. They may have been prompted because of David's complaints about his commute on the London Underground and his yearning for adventure, but it ended up being quite the adventure for the little ones. The plans made involved each child carrying their own rucksack as we set out.

The eldest celebrated her ninth birthday at Bondi Beach. They rode horses across the sandy beaches in Fiji and saw dolphins in the wild in Kaikoura, New Zealand. They got to travel in a cable car to Sentosa Island in Singapore, go to war museums in Vietnam, roller-skate along Venice Beach, go to Gold's Gym in Santa Monica, bask in the culture of the Te Papa Tongarewa Museum of Wellington, enjoy the scenery of Auckland, see the stars on the pavement along the Hollywood Walk of Fame, let off paper lanterns in the temples of Thailand, and even see actual bats flying in the Australian night sky, as well as go inside the Sydney Opera House, where my daughters were especially impressed by the washbasins in the restrooms.

At times, things got a bit sketchy. In Australia, I got conned into booking an apartment overlooking the beach. The actual accommodation was in stark contrast to the foyer area, and I had to strip the beds and lay our own clothes on the mattresses for the kids to rest. I sat in a chair the entire night holding my youngest son. The next day, I found more legit and hygienic lodgings down the road.

It was an exhilarating adventure of escapism. We were together, at least me and the kids. But after a three-month stint 'round the globe, we returned to South Africa so I could work again. Money could only stretch so far.

The marriage eventually crumbled three years later, and I had to start all over again, this time with three kids.

CHAPTER 6

All the Way
to Being Blindsided

#roundandround

'The wound is the place where the light enters you.'

RUMI

NO MATTER WHERE WE LIVED DURING MY FIRST MARRIAGE, my home was always an extension of me. I loved tasteful pieces, but practicality was important. I never had a show house that was pristine with ostentatious furniture. Instead, it boasted an eclectic style infused with comforts. Luxury comforts. Large sofas, lots of cushions, paintings, and family photos galore.

Oh, and I loved to buy stuff. Stuff for the house. Stuff for the kids. Stuff for others. Stuff for me. I love bags and shoes. What woman doesn't? I mean, one's shoe size never fluctuates, does it? Once a size five always a size five, unlike my weight. At one point, my daughters had over 180 stuffed toys and all sorts of other crap. My son had over 100 toy cars by the time he was a year old, and I had close to 120 pairs of shoes. Who the fuck needs 180 stuffed toys and 120 pairs of shoes? Things and more things to distract from that missing *thingy-me-bop*.

Even when I couldn't afford things, I'd cook grandiose meals with limited groceries of potatoes and eggs, always performing for myself. Never forgoing two-ply toilet paper. I was Miss Pretty Little Thing trying to live her best life, but it wasn't by a long shot. I chased perfection. I wanted to be the perfect wife, sister, daughter, and most of all, mother, but I was drowning. Still, I threw myself into the children's lives, making sure that they had more than they needed, pursuing daily extramural activities which they desired, from swimming and gymnastics to football and horse riding to drama and piano lessons. Whenever we moved, settling the kids into their new rooms and decorating was such a satisfying accomplishment, momentarily fulfilling, as I proved to myself that I was capable of it all.

As I continued fooling myself that my life was fulfilling and my children had what they needed as long as we had a two-parent home, underneath it all there was still that sense of unworthiness, a need to prove I could do certain things others wouldn't dare to do. Like uprooting their family time and time again, the adrenaline rush of a new adventure, taking leaps of faith like the fool in the tarot deck. This was all subconscious.

I was trying to fix it all. Driven by ego, I also needed to prove that I could hold a marriage together and still be an independent woman. But I was tired. Inside, there was a huge gaping hole. That goddamn *thingy* was still missing.

Keeping myself busy was my survival, all the while neither thriving nor living but doing what was traditionally expected of me and finding whatever joy I could in mundane tasks. The sense of the missing *thingy* festered and grew as days slipped into weeks, then into months and into years, and eventually decades.

An eternal optimist, I believe in always seeing the glass half full. Who knows what will happen, eh? Gotta keep the faith and vibrations high. You're only supposed to fall in love three times apparently, first with a soulmate, then in a karmic relationship, and then with your twin flame. 'Third time lucky' is my mantra. Maybe that's true, maybe not, but three has always been my lucky number. Unfortunately, I wasn't to three yet. I still had to go through two.

Erroneously, I still believed happiness could only be achieved if two people pulled together in raising a family. I was a free thinker compared to most people I knew, but societal norms were still deeply ingrained. I actually thought my daughters needed a father figure in their lives to eradicate daddy issues and that my son needed a male role model to show him the way forward. I believed my choice not to sustain my first marriage was a failing, and so I needed to fix it for them.

I never paused to think how the concept of the traditional family became part of my psyche and beliefs. It would take me quite a bit more time to realise that self-love is the only essential ingredient in all things. Yet, I followed this indoctrinated falsehood, believing 'it's the right thing to do.' Consequently, I hurled myself into a second marriage to fit the ideal family dynamic within society, no matter what that meant for me.

ROSE-TINTED GLASSES

I met the man who would become my second husband at the gym. We'll call him Mark. He had combed back inky-black hair. Each thinning strand meticulously combed to disguise his receding hairline using a toothbrush. Yes, yes, he used a toothbrush. Who uses a toothbrush on their hair? Except those who need to sort their edges. But here he was using a toothbrush. I sneaked up on him and saw him staring in the mirror with his head tilted, toothbrush at the ready (eye roll), but I didn't want to be judgy.

It was a distinct sign, perhaps. A joke from my guardian angel— who knows I can be quite critical—yet in this scenario, I chose not to be. Mark boasted a lean physique and an awkward goofy demeanour with close-set blue eyes. I only knew his eyes were blue about four years later when my daughter mentioned it in passing. Hard to believe, I know, but clearly, I was not present whenever I 'looked' into his eyes. I was living mindlessly and didn't know it. I found him odd but kind, eager to please, a definite allure to my ego. Not my usual type. In fact, neither was my first husband. I tend to like a bit of rough. A bit of a bad boy with a stank attitude. A bit of a cheeky chappy who makes me roll with laughter because he's so smooth with his comebacks. I listened to Shaggy's music a lot in my teens, catch my drift? I like confidence, not arrogance. I like thug, but one who doesn't take people for mugs and who actually has a legitimate business. I like a tough guy with a teddy-bear heart. Tupac with a lot of spiritual vibes added in. Summed up as the three Ss'—Street, Swagger and Spirituality.

Mark was certainly no Tupac. But he was rugged, pleasant, and heeded my unusual request to be a personal trainer to my three children—eleven, nine, and five at the time. I was on a mission to get my pizza-loving clan to cultivate healthier habits. I was a working mum, after all, and often opted for takeaways of their choice to ease the guilt. Hopefully, Mark could help since David was certainly not the athletic type back then. What we did have were the financial resources for the kids to be trained, so we thought, *Why not?*

My marriage to David was now friend-zoned and arguments were fierce and often. We were both unhappy and resentful and threw ourselves into our respective careers. Things were so bad that the driver who would ferry the children to their private school was thought to be my husband as he and I were the only faces seen at the school. David was totally immersed in work, and family time was minimal. The driver was tall, a rugby player and came from the flats with immense street connections. I enjoyed his mentorship over the children as he was kind but with sharp street smarts.

The marriage to David hit rock bottom. I was studying, yet again, to enhance my future growth, and he was incensed that I chose to go out with some girlfriends one night. The next morning, the usually passive David was filled with such rage that he kicked the side mirror of my car while the kids were strapped in the back. I knew there was no going back. I had been here before in previous relationships, and although I knew he would not be abusive as previous partners, the fact that he was violent in front of the kids hurt. This was the pinnacle of countless months of nastiness between us and endless nights of arguing and keeping me awake in his induced state. It had now erupted. David and I were merely ships passing in the night. We couldn't pull it together. Our egos clashing, our needs unmet, our desires unfulfilled.

In hindsight, it is quite unpalatable that we opted for a personal trainer rather than a simple walk in a park or a bike ride to get the children's lazy arses up and out. We were that far apart. But Mark was dutiful and had a military background that appealed to my alpha male illusion of who he might be.

As David and I battled in divorce court, he soon moved to a different city, leaving me with the children. He dutifully paid child maintenance but contact, while they were little, was sparse.

Soon enough, Mark had crept into my heart, announcing eight months later to my children that he was in love with me. He was handy. For one, he drove us everywhere. Two, he was tall. I let the fact that I could not have deep conversations with him, like I had with David, slide. *Can't have everything* I thought, and he was great with the kids—keeping them active and all that. Soon enough would come the proposal with a ring. All too good to be true, like in a movie…and it was…all too good to be true. Mark, too, had issues, which soon became apparent. Sure, he could re-enact bits and pieces from movies he had watched—his bids to be the 'man he was supposed to be.' A somebody who people admired just like the fathers he saw in movies. But it was all make-believe for him, for me, for us.

Mark was one year younger than me but looked older, much older. He had salt-and-pepper hair and worked as a mercenary on occasion. Having been previously married, he had a son, whom he hardly saw. This rang instant alarm bells, but I chose to cover my ears. David also had a son he had hardly seen. I didn't dig for answers with either man. Instead, I believed Mark's sob story that he was being denied access to his son by a vindictive ex. The exact tactic he would later employ against me during our custody battle. It was during our court case that I mustered up the courage to speak to his first wife who, unsurprised by my battle with him, informed me that he'd had no contact with his son, nor had he paid any child maintenance, for more than a decade. But the Mark prior to our divorce was attentive and enthusiastic in his role as a father figure to my three children from David.

Our romance flourished quickly as he was protective and loving. And he bloody drove a car. (The car thing was a bonus as I'd been the sole driver throughout my thirteen-year first marriage and I was, frankly, bloody exhausted.) So instead of vetting him properly and giving it time, I was so thrilled with the little things. Let me reiterate, the man actually drove a car. It reminded me of my high school days when my boyfriends came to collect me in their souped-up Ford with mag wheels, tinted windows, sunroof, and spoilers. Mark helped with ferrying the children, and although less cerebral than David, he seemed more family-orientated, happy to taxi the children wherever they desired. He even taught my eldest son to play cricket, football, and to ride a bicycle. The attention he bestowed on my kids was priceless, allowing me to turn a blind eye to his meagre income and controlling ways.

He nervously proposed to me on bended knee at the beach. I accepted even though I was leaving in a month with my children—without him—to spend time in Beijing. The kids needed to learn Mandarin, and I was tired of Cape Town. My Boeta had created an opportunity for me, and I loved a new adventure in foreign lands.

Subconsciously, the pattern of running from myself was repeating itself. I convinced myself that the trip to China would see me helping the family printing business as I would investigate opportunities in this arena, being the former and youngest female chairperson of a printing and publishing operation. It seemed like an ideal time to uproot before plunging into a second marriage. I wanted the children to feel secure that they would always come first, so a Beijing adventure without my fiancé was a no-brainer. Kids first, fiancé second, that is how I rolled. Kids before dicks. The girls were teenagers, and my son, at the time, was a pre-teen, so I wanted time to bond alone with them. Anyway, Mark was a grown-ass man and could fend for himself, and if the love was strong enough, then there would be no objection from him.

The kids and I flew out to spend an entire year on our own without him and then we would tie the knot. I was comfortable with a long-distance relationship, as I believed that we had forged a solid foundation of trust and had no concerns at all. I was mesmerised by China's capital, the culture, the people, and the hustle and bustle. After eight months in Beijing alone with the children, we returned so I could marry in Cape Town. I remotely planned the blue-and-white-themed yacht wedding, which would host a close group of no more than sixty people to celebrate our union. Heartfelt speeches reduced everyone to tears. The love and support from others was palatable. The children were central in the celebrations, and I was happy. Soon after, we would return to Beijing.

Truth be told, I had cold feet the night before the wedding and suggested that perhaps we just have a union of promise. He reminded me he needed a spousal visa for China if he was to join us. *Oh crap.* I'd forgotten about that. Four months after tying the knot, he joined us, and we ended up staying five years in total. Before he arrived, I had enjoyed being on my own. I missed him on occasion, but it wasn't like I wanted him around daily other than to help out with the children. Another red flag.

Baby 4

CODEPENDENCY AND MANIPULATION

Mark appeared docile, while I was the feisty, fiery one, but in reality, he was a master manipulator. I did not suspect a thing. No one did—until the proverbial shit hit the fan. A covert narcissist, able to be both victim and perpetrator rolled into one, Mark knew how to elicit sympathy from me with floods of tears about how he felt he was not good enough for me—revealing that was why he was incessantly jealous, not wanting me to have male friends—how I deserved better than him; how his love for me was all-consuming; how he needed me; and how he would have no reason to live without me and the children.

Looking back, I can see everything clearly. Even when I was in Beijing on my own for an entire year, I went out only thrice because he would call every night at random times to check in. I was also under the illusion that by me going out and having fun, I would feed his insecurities, and that would somehow be unfair to him. He would often share how broken he was. At first, I admired his open vulnerability, but as the years rolled on, him being a loner and unable to self-soothe would be the catalyst for an unhealthy codependency. Although I was always geared to please, the enormity of having to feed his ego and soothe his pain became overwhelming. It made me feel more and more inadequate that I could not make him feel good about himself.

As time progressed, Mark became accustomed to being energetically fed by my positive reassurances rendering me energetically depleted and resentful. He yearned to be the centre of my world, but my children were always my priority. Never once did I favour a romantic weekend without my trio tagging along. It was how I believed I could remedy any abandonment issues they may have felt by not having their biological father around. My former husband was both distant to them emotionally and physically. Internally, I still felt the guilt of initiating the divorce. If I wanted to go out on my own, Mark would want to know why I didn't prefer to be home and close to him. It triggered the neglect he felt as a child, he would say. Being an empath, of course, I would soothe him and forgo my own 'selfish' desires of wanting to be sociable.

My fourth child, a boy, was born in the cold winter of Beijing. When I was younger, I'd always vowed that I would never have children from two different men, but obviously, the Universe listened and voilà, my harsh judgements came home to roost. Mark taught English in Beijing, which didn't bring in much, and the savings I had so diligently accumulated while we were apart dwindled with an extra mouth to feed. I was working in marketing at a Chinese-owned private hospital and was a contributing writer and on the editorial board of *Beijing Kids*, a popular magazine geared towards expat families. Eventually, it was time to return home to England. My daughters, now fluent in Mandarin, left for England first. A year prior to us leaving with both my sons. Plans were put in place that Mark would return to Africa to work while I, yet again, worked on his spousal visa so he could live in England with us.

It took just over a year for us to be reunited again, but it was far from magical. Cracks were already evident in Beijing. In fact, cracks were evident before we even tied the knot, but I chose to just readjust those rose-tinted glasses and give the smudges a clean. I talked myself out of feeling stifled with him around, convincing myself that I'd only need to build him up a bit to ease his control. After all, it was good for the kids to have a father figure and for me to have someone with potential. Always the potential thing we, as women, sometimes bandy about. This guy I'm with is not a total loser; he has potential, right?

After my oldest daughter left to attend university and the second left for private schooling in England, it was only Mark, the boys, and me in Beijing. Soon enough, he was getting on my bloody nerves, and the flight to England could not come soon enough. His controlling ways were becoming more and more isolating.

His reach into my mind was so rooted that even when I was in England, I could not seem to escape the control he exerted. Whilst in England celebrating my milestone fortieth birthday, my daughter hired a fun butler in the buff, and I had all my girlfriends 'round to my new home. A butler in the buff is a good-looking bloke who strips and is there for you and your whooping friends to enjoy. Boxers retained but rippling muscles and abs on full glistening display while serving you drinks and hors d'oeuvres. Well, the photographs on Facebook triggered him, and I was accused of being disrespectful and not behaving like a wife should. Wtf?! It wasn't the first time it was communicated that I was cheating or undermining him. Needless to say, the marriage disintegrated month after month, exacerbated by his insane jealousy. But still, I believed if we were reunited as a family we could survive. These days, I have no social media bar IG because of him, and that's private now.

Finally, I secured his spousal visa for England. We all waited for him to join us—when the unexpected happened. He cancelled his flight and sent a text message that he was being blackmailed because he'd been sexting someone. What the hell?! How? Why? Yet again, my world crumbled. After years of over-giving, once again I was the one being hurt. And to make matters worse, four kids were going to be adversely affected by all this shit. Eventually, he did fly over, ready with an apology. But when he landed, it all turned to shit. The sexting admission was just the tip of the mountain of shite.

It was dark. An inky, suffocating kind of dark. Velvet nights were displaced by crimson confusion as details unfolded beyond the sexting. Memories of evenings past were now no longer sultry nor seductive. Swatches of intimate moments now rigorously repainted in my mind's eye. Violations within the marriage echoed in bloody lips and spiky stilettos. I could taste remnants of puke stuck at the back of my throat as he spoke. The crust of projectile vomit stuck on my lips. I sank overwhelmed, exhausted, and spent into the softness of my down duvet that evening of September 2017. My emotions were as crumpled as the bedding on my king-size bed. My head was throbbing, eyelids swollen—now clamped shut. My throat was hoarse from yelling. Body rigid. How did this happen? How could I have been so blind? So stupid?

The truth is, I had no inkling. I was blindsided. Urban Dictionary definition: *A scenario where everything breaks, normally happening out of nowhere.* My significant other, the love of my life, sucker-punched me. I braced and then succumbed to the imminent terror of his words. The final horror: 'It wasn't just…sexting.' He stood sheepishly at the side of the bed with that stance he had held many times before, when he was confessing to not having money or that his parents needed financial help. His head hung low, and he had tears in his eyes.

How could this be? He had only just landed in England a few hours earlier, a spousal visa securing his entry. And here we were in what was supposed to be our forever home. The home I had painstakingly renovated, ripping out floors with my older son, remodelling the kitchen, envisaging happy family gatherings, ensuring there were bedrooms for each of the kids and enough family room for us all to congregate. The older children sensed the tension and left for a long walk. They took their youngest sibling along to protect him from the incoming eruption, which was guaranteed. They could see how my initial excitement about him joining us had evaporated.

A mere week prior, I had finally gathered some excitement about him returning. Now, that had all dissipated to a simmering anger. The cake, which I had baked with my youngest son, and the carefully iced welcome home message had been changed to *welcome home, cheater*. In the lead-up to his arrival, I was like a wounded wild animal, unexpectedly caught in a trap. The iron jaws of the trap were now tearing at my flesh as I struggled against the unexpected betrayal.

His return was the final blow to our union, and I knew it. I knew that this home—the pinnacle of our family dream, our new beginning—was about to be demolished. Wasn't it a mere six years ago now, on Valentine's Day, that we spoke about love, new beginnings, and a fresh start for two people who both had previous heartbreaks? Clearly, I was only stacking brick upon brick on a foundation that was not as stable as I had thought.

HINDSIGHT IS 20/20

Our intimate wedding in 2010 had heralded a perfect blended family, a momentous merger born from brokenness—so I thought at the time. But what I attracted was a reflection of my own brokenness. This was not love. In hindsight, this was a trauma bond with a man I didn't truly know. I loved the idea of him being a father figure. I loved the illusion of him being a family man, which he fed through his diligent ferrying of the kids everywhere and anywhere.

My poor children had sung their hearts out at the wedding. My shy son supported by his older sister after practising the *Beauty and the Beast* song for weeks on end. My youngest daughter sang a beautiful solo, too. I had felt so proud and glad that they felt part of this new beginning. This was our chance at happiness. Their biological dad had also remarried, and they were not included in his nuptials, which made mine all the more meaningful. The blue and white balloons and the three-tier white chocolate wedding cake adorned with seashells enhanced the ocean atmosphere aboard the yacht. I had always wanted to get married on a yacht. We even saw a whale near the yacht, an unusual sighting, and I felt my Dadda's presence strongly. I was happy.

What I didn't know is that Mark had many secrets. Secrets that enveloped his own brokenness. Secrets that made him incapable of loving me the way I expected him to. How could he? He didn't love himself. How could I receive a healthy love when I, too, didn't love myself? If I had, I would have seen more clearly, made fewer excuses for his intense jealousy and controlling traits. If I'd had more self-love, I would have believed I was indeed worthy of not being controlled, not being isolated, and not being made to have to prove myself day in and day out. Simply put, I would have had boundaries on how I should be treated. Without strong boundaries, I was inevitably bounding towards another disaster of my own making.

CONFESSIONS CONFIDENTIAL

Now, here I am in England with the man confessing all, and the illusion is cruelly and coldly dissipating. 'I don't know what's wrong with me,' he goes on, 'but I just can't help it. I still love you. You have to believe that.' He bends over and inches closer. *Which part can't you help? The pathology of lies or the prowling?* I wonder. He stretches his hand out and attempts to stroke my hair. I glimpse his titanium wedding band with the bespoke swivel centre. It was specially crafted to accommodate his habit of swivelling rings between his thumb and forefinger. I flinch at his touch. My arms and hands cover my head as I attempt to shield myself from the bombs of truth raining from the rose-tinted sky. I muffle my anguished moans as I gasp for air. The front door clicks shut downstairs. *Has three hours passed already?* The kids said they would be out for at least that amount of time. My mind bounces between the searing pain and sadness I feel as a woman and a mother who cannot let them know. *I mustn't let the children hear. I mustn't let the children see.*

Despite repeatedly chanting this, I cannot contain the shock and pain as it rips through me in the aftermath of the blast. 'Prostitutes.' His lips are moving, but I can't hear anything anymore. Feelings of shame descend around me. Helplessness closing in from all four walls. Is he trying to convince me of a lapse in judgement? A slip-up? I catch the tail end: 'I will do anything, whatever it takes, to make this right, to save our family,' he says.

The stillness I sought after divorcing David is gone. The happiness and dreamy delight at meeting Mark, shattered. My eternal quest for inner peace, through sporadic yoga and qigong, obliterated. My endeavours to meditate evaporate wispily. Mindfulness becomes madness. Dirty, dark, desperate, debilitating delirium. I'm dripping, perspiring profusely. 'Be present,' say the yogis. 'It's a gift.' Well, if this is what being present means, then it's a truly shitty gift. There's nothing special or unusual about my pain; I know it hasn't only happened to me. Cheating is common, infidelity infinite in this world we live in. But knowing this does nothing to stem feelings of utter shock at the cruelty and unfairness of it all. My belief that I am winning emotionally, in family, in life, in love, is now gone.

I notice that my grey T-shirt clings to my huddled frame. My armpits sodden despite the crisp autumn chill outside. Storm clouds fill the East Sussex sky and descend low on the horizon. Cliff tops beckoning, crashing waves calling. I love gazing at the sea from my bedside window. It's the key reason I chose this house and made it home. Panoramic views of sea and downland, the unobstructed potential of life itself. Tears crawl down my cheeks, crashing like salty waves, smudging with the sweat on my clammy body. A hot furnace fuelled by confusion swells within me.

My heart rapidly palpitates. I grab my tightening chest. Vitriolic anger snakes unexpectedly through me amid a symphony of searing sadness. I feel hate and disgust for him, for myself, confused in an orchestra of pity and emptiness. Mid-forties, four children, two husbands, Africa, Asia, and one dreary island later, here I am. Lonely and mournful at a graveside of broken dreams. Did I mention I am forty-five years old and feeling every goddamn year of that suffocating age? Did I mention that when I love I'm all in? I remind myself that I've always seen the glass half full rather than half empty, but years of not being enough to myself or anyone else is forcing me to face the crossroads of life in all its glory.

Am I strong enough to say I won't save you at the expense of myself? Or will I again sacrifice my wholeness to make you whole again? My gaze drifts toward the fog descending across the English Channel, back to a childhood peppered with happy and not-so-happy memories. Back to a mother whose pain I witnessed. Back to a father who I loathed, yet somehow also loved and excused.

Breathe, I say to myself. *Fucking breathe.*

WORKING WITH
PERVASIVE ADDICTION

The next day, after hardly any sleep, I felt empty. Blank. Belittled. Broken. My bedside pedestals awkwardly accommodated two oversize crystal lamps precariously perched between rows of bottled perfume and bubblegum wrappers. 'I'm really sorry' were his morning utterances as I sat stony-faced, cross-legged on my bed, propped uncomfortably against the wooden headboard. I grabbed my mobile. I followed my finger to the fourth number scribbled on the piece of paper balanced on my leg. I was in full fix-it mode. Deliriously intent on making this fucked-up situation right.

'Hello…yes, can you please help me?' Fresh tears flowed. Mucous mingled with salty spray.

'Can you please help me? My husband. He just confessed to seeing prostitutes. Please help me fix this, fix him.'

I looked over at him and saw his eyes glistening from the constant onslaught of tears. Dark circles and wrinkles framed what was no longer a piercing blue but, rather, a vacant grey pair of eyes. His hair a dull grey in the sunlight creeping through the double-fronted windows. Who was this man before me? I get to know details now, more than I ever did when we were together. I learnt that he was raised in a poor white family. That he had an alcoholic father who regularly beat him and his brothers. That his mother is of mixed heritage but ardently refuses to admit to it and sees the mix as dirty blood.

Therapy unearthed that his mother was routinely slapped till his parents found God. That the balance of power in his parents' marriage was as uneven as in my own parents' union. Therapy showed me how codependent I was on wanting to save and fix situations that were not mine to fix. It showed that I was not responsible for Mark's sexual addiction and that it was something only he could navigate—and only if he wanted to. My work was to unpack my own childhood trauma and not be held hostage to his recovery. I wanted him to be a healthy father to our son, but that was his choice to make. All I could do was work on me. He admitted that his first wife ran away from him because of his stifling control. Despite this admission, he quickly reverted back to his father's choices of abuse, quietly adding, 'I will never ever hit a woman.' He had told me, Real men don't. I respect you.' His words were well-rehearsed. Now in therapy, his words felt empty. 'What I did was wrong, but I'm sorry. I can fight this addiction. I know I can.'

Everyone who met Mark found him charming. A decent bloke. *A good egg*, as they'd say in England. Friends had a renewed faith in love as they observed us. Their cynical views on love and marriage momentarily dispelled by my obvious happiness and his attentiveness. His strong arms would hold me close in our giddy courting days as he whispered, 'You will always be safe. I love you.' I remember holding on tight, sniffing the musky cologne, daring to believe in love again. Daring to believe devotion from another was possible. I was missing devotion to myself, though.

Now here we were in the confines of a therapy room. The therapist, who we'll call Trish, had a comforting voice as she urged us to come in. She had calmed me when I had called her the day before. She created space in her schedule and saw us in crisis. She was kind. It was in her eyes. Her smile was gentle, too. I needed gentleness. I needed consoling. The room walls were painted in a choice cream colour akin to a faint vanilla custard. Not garish but serene. A brown wooden desk sat against one wall. On the other, an unused fireplace with wax candles. They were unlit. There were rows and rows of books on the shelf behind her as she sat in a comfy chair opposite us.

I was nervous. Thank God for that bichon frisé. Oh, how I loved that Trish had a dog. 'Now that you remember what made you fall in love, separate the man from the addiction,' she said. She guided me through the most painful betrayal, unpacking the intricacies of sex addiction.

'Addicts can choose to change behaviour and retrain the neural pathways of their brain. This can be a safe space for him to offload indiscretions and shake off shame, which is so closely aligned with all addiction.' She empathised, yet effectively explained it all. My brain was overloaded, but I was determined to gain an understanding as to why it happened. Mark embraced the process of outing his double life, and I was happy for his release. But I never managed the sensory overload, the ability to practise mindfulness in the midst of triggering information. Stereotypical whores in short skirts with large bosoms burst forth blurry, burning my brain.

He was good at releasing it all. Week in and week out. First, ten confessions. Then one hundred. Then too many to count. Confessions were staggered, spanning over days, weeks, months. Red-and-black images in a kaleidoscope of unrelenting pain. With each turn of the instrument, I saw my wedding overlap with a dingy room and dirty sheets. The John, zipping up his trousers before uttering, 'I do' the following day in front of our family and friends. Memories of being pregnant at forty in China. I would listen, aghast, to stories retold by locals and *laowai* involving bustling brothels and married foreigners. Was he, indeed, one of those married foreigners?

Seven years together were unpacked in seven months of therapy. Trish never dictated but guided the process until I came to the realisation that the truth was elusive. That the path I sought to uncover and understand was not mine to travel. My journey was not to save the addict but to save myself. And through this entire process, there was not a word or a check-in from my family. It all took its toll on me. I felt more alone than ever. I felt like the fucking loser version of the Lone Ranger, unable to fucking load up as I usually did and certainly unable to take aim and fire at anyone. I was defeated.

I tried to refocus during yet another battering of a confession as the walls closed in. How he used my car to pick up hookers. How he prowled for a fix in the dead of night during a family trip. How he had affairs with work colleagues. I contacted some of these colleagues both in Beijing and in Cape Town. It turned out that his confessions were untrue. He was simply adding more fuckery. It was impossible to fathom why someone would do that. Why add on to what was already an appalling set of infidelities? He had already made me aware of the advertisements. *Married man seeking fun. No strings attached.* Sexting whoever, whenever as a gesture of zero fucks given to the unseen. An unrelenting projection of images heralded by a cacophony of cackles and pitiful stares saturated my exploding head. I wanted to dull the pain, drown the images, stifle the panic, and somehow eradicate the emptiness.

Enter Trish with an explanation for the constant changing stories—for some sense of the method behind the madness. She explained that it was because an addict's shame is huge. The pathology of lies are normal to cover the shame or add to it because of the addict's innate sense of unworthiness coupled with inadequacy. 'He loved you as much as he could,' she said in one session. This truth hit home. It hit hard. And I knew then that I was at a crossroads. Forge ahead in this quagmire of shit in which my kids and I were collateral damage, or heal from it.

In the midst of all this crap, I eventually received a call from my brother, my Boeta. He'd had a crisis of his own, and he called frantic. His mistress, who he had taken great lengths to hide, had been uncovered. I didn't mention how the duality of his life added to my own anguish. Instead, I listened and advised. His baby mamma called later, and I did the same: calmed the tears, shared advice. At least she had the temerity to listen briefly to my pain before focusing on hers. But here I was again, placing my needs second in an effort to fix them.

My mind was not my own during those days. It could switch from focusing on peeling a potato to a narrative of a punter who perceived family time together as an equal exchange for a release in the rear of a car amid baby seats and kids' books. My mind was out of control. I had never blinked at the classifieds in newspapers. Now I was obsessed with perusing them while I swigged vodka. I drank every evening when the kids were in bed. May have been two weeks straight. I smoked up to two packs of cigarettes a day. I wanted details. I wanted dates and times. I wanted to know if the money he asked for was for mobile internet service or blow jobs. Obviously, he needed the internet data not to check up on the family but also to book a sex session. Over and over again, I frantically dissected every moment he was out of my sight. It was impossible to decipher what was true and what was a lie. The therapist reassured me that this was normal behaviour of the party who has been cheated on. Nothing was normal to me anymore. Nothing seemed worth living for anymore. I felt nothing. Desired nothing. Just numbness.

Three hours of sleep per night, angry at myself for not seeing the red flags. Disgusted at myself for sleeping with him. Hating myself for promising my kids a blended family and fucking it up. Had I known he was a sex addict I would not have been with him. But then, it would not have been an addiction. It's not like people shout their addictions from the rooftops.

'Hey, wanna go out for a drink? And by the way, I'm addicted to heroin.'

'Hey, wanna hang out? Oh, and by the way, I'm an alcoholic.'

'Hey, there, would love to marry you, but I'm a sex addict.'

Therapy was helpful, and I even found a healer who did energy work. I took Mark and the kids, as I believed in both Western and Eastern healing. But even with the temporary relief of my reality, it always came crashing down. The healing I needed was not external, and I knew it. It was internal, and I needed it long before this travesty in my life. The path for me was the journey into self-love and purpose, not the infidelity. Spirit was only propelling me towards this by creating a crisis so huge in my life that I had no choice but to re-evaluate who I was, what I stood for, and where the heck I was heading.

There exists many debates around sex addiction: the causes and remedies for it. I choose not to go into it in this book, but no matter the method—what I can tell you is that none of it matters when you're in the thick of it all. I read so many books, watched so many videos, and had so many sessions, but you cannot help someone who does not choose to help themselves. Also, I could no longer distract myself by wanting to save my kids from this destruction as the damage was done. They were both hurt and angry. At him and at me. I was devastated. The time had come to fix *me*.

Through a journey of introspection, one can find hope, healing, and love. But it's a damn long road, and only the brave face these pains head on. Mark needed to go on his own journey, and so did I. If he wanted to heal, it would ultimately have to be his decision, not mine.

Some people simply choose the easier path of blame. Some use substances to dull life or choose to fix the other person and not themselves. Some find distractions, or they live in denial. Ultimately, the only way to heal is through the pain. I'll repeat that for those at the back. The only way to heal is through the pain, to embrace that mother fucker tightly. For only when you know darkness and accept it can you know what light truly is, what it means, and why you have to encompass both. For without one, the other cannot exist. This is the beauty of the duality of all of existence, all wondrously encapsulated in all that you are and in all that I am.

WHEN IT ALL FINALLY ENDED

During this time of trying to piece life back together, I could hardly drag myself out of bed. I wanted to stay under the duvet where it was dark and safe. But I still had to get Alfie, the youngest, to school. He needed that normality, that routine. Most days, everything else was a blur until I collected Alfie from school and prepared dinner. Then there was my eldest son who witnessed it all, and my heart broke for him. I had fucked up so badly I was being consumed by guilt that I chose this man as a father figure. I couldn't forgive myself for inflicting this pain on my kids. I internalised the blame for a long time, using Mark's addiction as an excuse for his behaviour. That he needed help, not judgement. I was trying to avoid the pain of being judged by my own kids. I was an ultimate failure as a mum. I never kept them emotionally safe despite my intentions—wanting to create the best family life for them—I screwed it up, and I was to blame. Again, Trish reiterated that to internalise the guilt and blame would not bode well for my healing. The self-loathing was huge.

Mark was unemployed, so he was around, and there was a deafening silence between us. I was consumed by wanting to know the truth, and he agreed to a polygraph test to ascertain whether he cheated whilst I was pregnant. He was adamant that he did not. The test proved otherwise, but none of it really mattered in the end. Days blended into nights. I imagined this was how functioning addicts survived. I was able to compartmentalise being a mother when I needed to be and then slump back into a no man's land of neurosis and numbness.

One evening, I urgently needed to escape the house. I sat in my car in the garage. I turned on the ignition and realised I'd run out of cigarettes, and it was 11:00 p.m. I knew the petrol station was still open this time of night, and as I fidgeted around in my car. I suddenly stopped. Emotional darkness descended around me. Self-loathing looking large. I felt empty, fucked-up empty, no feelings of wanting to carry on in this shitty life of mine. *Fuck, how does gassing myself in the car fucking work?* I thought to myself. I knew someone who had committed suicide in this way, but I couldn't even gather the strength to end it all. Bloody decisions: cigarettes or carbon monoxide? Slow or swift ending?

I just sat, staring out the windscreen at all the shit in my garage. In one corner, plastic crates of toys. In another, garden tools balancing precariously over the lawnmower and the garden hose. In a lucid moment, I considered my children. My sons, asleep in their beds. My daughters, now young women at university, who witnessed their mother divorce before and get back up and now was fucking back down again. What message would I be sending them if I let this keep me on the bloody floor? Hadn't they already suffered enough? How would they feel if I abandoned them, too? That thought was not so fleeting. Thank goodness it remained. It sat suspended between me, the car, and the exhaust pipe. I felt nauseous and confused. Exhausted and expired emotionally. The engine had been running for God knows how long, but eventually I pressed the remote to open the garage door. Finally, I reached for the seat belt. Best hurry as the garage shop would shut in a few minutes. Best get two packs of ciggies just in case.

Another time, I found myself on the pebbled beach, unaware of how I even got there. The ocean seemed so welcoming. *What if I just floated?* I thought as it started to rain again. I stripped down, and the cold air hit my skin. Soon enough, I was submerged under the icy water, holding my breath. *What if I just let go and let it flow?* I wondered. Gasping, I surfaced for air. *Shit, I've gone a bit from the shore, and I'm not a strong swimmer.* Fuckity fuck. I started to do something between a weak stroke, a doggie paddle, and a back float back to the pebbled shore.

Changing my mind in the midst of wanting to end it all made me realise how far I had allowed my emotions to control me. They were feelings, yes, but they did not need to consume me. I had the choice to focus on living and learning rather than on death and despair. The sobering thoughts of wanting to survive this trauma gushed over me as I bopped to shore and shivered in my wet underwear. I looked out to the horizon and contemplated my next move.

My next move was to say, *FUCK THIS!* I found a healthier outlet for my pain and anguish and joined a local Muay Thai gym. There, I could fuck things up. I could box and kick and regain my sense of power. I joined the gym nine days post shocker. Yes, I know what the experts say. Take three days to sulk, no more than seven days max, and then get your shit together. Well, I'm here to tell you it took me far longer. All in all, recovery took three years and remains a work in progress.

To this day, I am still going through a process of healing childhood wounds. But after three years, I could finally stop projecting fears of cheating onto every man I met, which seemed like an impossible feat when I began down this healing path. In fact, my trust issues extended beyond gender and extended to everyone. I second-guessed my choice of every person I interacted with on a daily basis.

The exercise and therapies were important steps in this path, and I continue to value these modalities for healing to this day. I turned down medication offered to me at various stages to either help me sleep or to reduce my anxiety. I was determined to have my mind control my emotions, and this I achieved through silence, through breath, through belief in me, and the murmurings of my guardian angels.

Once Mark completed therapy, our journeys continued separately. He vowed to continue his healing and give me and our son space, but I was still trapped in a cycle of fear and emotional abuse. A tightening of my stomach, a queasy feeling ever-present whenever he texted me to see his son. It was never simply about arrangements regarding contact; it always spiralled into old patterns of exerting control over me. I always felt guilty, internalising that I was not enough, not doing enough, not being supportive enough, not giving enough. While I accepted he could only love as deeply as he was capable of, I realised that I, too, could only love as deeply as I loved myself. And the truth was, I didn't love myself. And if I was ever going to have another relationship, I did not want it to form through another trauma bond or become codependency cloaked in an illusion of love.

So I mustered the strength to devote myself to me despite the barrage of text messages, which ensued many months after our therapy. Eventually, he agreed to divorce amicably, and I knew that he had many years of healing ahead. I needed to focus on me and my children yet again. I chose not to date; I didn't need unhealthy validation from sex escapades with different men. So celibacy it was, and two years eventually passed.

'You are vile and disgusting. You are not the mother I thought you were. I have no addiction. I was misdiagnosed. I will drag you through court again.' I was frozen with fright. A divorce finalised two years ago, now rebirthed after I tried to help him. The quote 'no good deed goes unpunished' came to mind. He had an agenda. He needed to renew his spousal visa. How could the family court not see his motivation? Frustrated tears caused the words to blur as they snarled at me from the screen. After months of trying to regain a semblance of normalcy in the home after his departure, the panic set in. The nausea became more distinct, eventually erupting into the toilet bowl as last night's chicken soup made an appearance. I gagged. I spluttered. I stuck my finger as far back as I could to release what refused to come up.

I was alone. Dadda was dead. Mamma, far away. Boeta, the businessman, unbothered. Sis, clueless.

I touched the cold sides of the toilet bowl, holding tightly, trying to decipher the venomous words spitting at me. Blindsided again. Coercive behaviour and gaslighting. Retraumatised and retriggered. Emotionally battered and bruised. No physical scars, no police report, no witnesses. Just a single snapshot of physical evidence. A blue and purple smattering of bruises etched symmetrically across both arms taken on my phone just prior to our divorce. Emotionally, I was held captive by a fear, which had repeatedly repainted across decades.

After a few moments, an angel with wings stolen from a phoenix defiantly arched across the canvas of my mind. I always believed in guardian angels, despite not being religious. I ardently believed in ancestral protection, and here it was. I whimpered tentatively, then boldly climbed the octane ladder of a scream. A lament of pain echoed through the empty house. As sudden as the scream started, it subsided. Self-love was defiant.

Vanilla musk permeated my nostrils from the scented candles. I breathed deeply. I loved the scent throughout the house. Vanilla bean reminded me of custard and love and light and calm. I remembered myself as a little girl sitting alone, waiting all those decades for someone—anyone—to save me. All grown up now, I reached over to my pedestal, unwrapped a Chappies bubble-gum and whispered at my reflection, 'I see you. I see you brave, brown-eyed girl. Speak.'

KEEPING IT 100

Two years after our first divorce, Mark dragged me to court again. A pathology of lies ensued during an arduous court process. It ended when he withdrew his petition and agreed to me relocating. I left for Cape Town in search of peace and solace. Yet, the trauma of it all remained. The only solace I had was that I was at least returning to where my two older siblings lived. Maybe I'd find some comfort there.

Being blindsided can happen anywhere, anytime, by anyone. Effectively executed by those in which you harbour the most faith. But in the bigger picture, we blindside ourselves. No one has that power over you unless you have relinquished it and so betrayed your own damn self. Yes, from a human earthly perspective, someone can do us wrong. But I had to change that perspective and look at things differently. I had to admit I did myself wrong.

It's not about them; their actions are their own, and their karma their own. Each of us must ultimately look inward at ourselves. My neediness made me marry this man, my longing for the traditional family, that which I internalised without question. I had good intentions. What I was wishing for was a happy family, but what I embraced instead was further dysfunction and inauthenticity.

There have been points along the way when I have not wanted to acknowledge what happened. I was often determined to dismiss it all, to shroud my hurt with non-plausible excuses and reduce the rejection to being a figment of my imagination. The truth was that I was hurt. Yet, my heart was still pumping, my eyes were still seeing, my ears were still hearing. I was feeling broken, but I was not ultimately broken. I still had the choice to heal and to rise. And that was what I did. The inspiring words of Maya Angelou come to mind: 'You may tread me in the very dirt but still, like dust, I'll rise.'

CHAPTER 7

A Spiritual Journey

#gratitudeattitude

'Hope is being able to see that there is light despite all of the darkness.'

DESMOND TUTU

TODAY, I HAVE COME TO THE TRUTH THAT THE UNIVERSE knew what it was doing all along the way. It was teaching me a twofold lesson. First, it was showing me that the words I had spoken many years earlier would manifest. What you think, what you speak, and what you believe is what you receive. I understand that now. My voice is my grace, simultaneously manifesting that which I speak.

Prior to my second marriage exploding in a spectacular fashion, I remember having a random conversation with my girlfriend while still married to David. She and I were close, trapped in a suburban lifestyle of fancy houses, fancy cars, and fancy schools. But we were rebels at heart, enjoying all the frills but understanding intrinsically that they did not define who we were.

While our children were being educated at private schools, we often reminisced of our own childhoods which were far simpler and modest. I would go so far as to state that what our children were experiencing was so far removed from what we had ever imagined was possible. When we were their age, we thought an outing to the beach was magical, a train ride was exciting, seeing relatives who came to visit was special. In contrast, our children were accustomed to long-haul flights to exotic destinations that our parents never dreamed of and definitely could never afford. Our kids saw restaurant meals as normal—I had never been to a restaurant until I was a working woman. Whereas I ate peanut butter sandwiches, they ate sushi. It's not that the children we raised didn't have hard times. They did. When they were young, there were times they ate boiled pasta, no sauce, for months on end as we penny-pinched. At times, they looked longingly at other kids spending tuck shop money while they had zero, and they were accustomed to second-hand uniforms while others brandished spanking-new outfits.

Emotionally, things were hard, too, as they witnessed their parents' coldness, brutal fights about money, and an overall sense of despair. So when we did have the funds, nothing was off limits for them. We overcompensate for many things devoid in our lives, both present day while raising them and in our frugal childhoods.

On this particular day, we were complaining about the banalities of our lives, despite the material benefits, and we wondered how the hell we found ourselves mindlessly moving through our daily routines. As usual, we had several hours to spare before the usual school run, so we went to our favourite hangout, which was a grandiose boutique hotel that had a delightful lounge area overlooking the green lawns and palm trees of the retreat. This gem of a place was round the corner from the children's school, and our kids were friends, so it was a common occurrence for us to meet here before the school pickup. On occasion, we would drop off, swing 'round the corner where she would park her Maserati next to my SUV, and we would have breakfast, lunch, and coffee before pickup. On this occasion, we poured ourselves copious cups of coffee and settled into our comfy winged armchairs dragging on what was likely our tenth ciggie. The owner joined us briefly for a cigarette and added that the next round of coffee would be on the house. As she left, our conversation turned to 'So what is worse, an affair or a one-night stand?'

The question sat there, hovering above us as we carefully contemplated our answer. Quick off the mark I chirped, 'Jesus, obviously a long-term affair would be more devastating as that would mean there are emotions involved. But I'd say a prostitute is better than a one-night stand. Like a garage. You pull up, fill up, and go.' Raucous laughter ensued as we stubbed out our fags and perfumed ourselves. 'Yes, no feelings involved. That's always better,' I said confidently.

And so it was—she and I agreed that our marriages and the dreariness of it all was as good as it got. Unconscious and so unaware were we that our voice was our power. We had just spoken that which would become my reality years later. Where energy flows is where the Universe goes. And so it was that the Universe balanced out matters, so to speak.

It is our duty as souls incarnate to revere the laws of Spirit, whether we believe or not. For Spirit is omnipotent, hearing and seeing everything. And through it all, we have a choice—to be conscious and mindful of what we utter or to unconsciously drift through life blaming circumstances and others for where we find ourselves. Now don't get it twisted. It doesn't mean I was solely responsible for what transpired in my life. My husbands had choices, too. It only means that the Universe hears every breath uttered and, without judgement, it manifests that which is thought and spoken. My voice was my power, and the truth of that came home to roost energetically at my doorstep in 2016, almost a decade later. I contributed to my own demise, but on the flip side, the aftermath and painstaking healing eventually helped me to rise towards faith and myself.

The second lesson the Universe taught me was to not let ego get in the way. Both hubbies were a mismatch for me and probably me for them. I prided myself on securing someone with an actual career during the first round of nuptials, and the second time 'round prided myself on not judging his humble beginnings. Both times, my actions were ego-driven, which kept me from seeing the truth. First time 'round I was thrilled that we both wanted to travel, and second time 'round I was thrilled he wanted to ferry the kids around and loved the concept of family. OMG. Both illusions. The former wanted to travel alright, but on his own if our around-the-world trip was anything to gauge events by. The latter ferried the kids around to fulfil his Oscar performance on what constitutes family. His desire to be a good parent and role model propelled by his own dysfunctional childhood and physical and emotional trauma.

I basked in Mark's resolute focus on me, unaware that the constant preoccupation of where I was and what I was doing had nothing to do with love and everything to do with control. Being in my mid-thirties, one would think that I was a woman who should've had ample experience. I should've spotted the red flags as I had been in an abusive relationship before David. But nothing could quell my naivety coupled with my romanticised illusions. I was incapable of recognizing green flags, never mind red flags, of a partner who is either overtly passive aggressive or covertly narcissistic.

When I trekked to Beijing with three kids and perhaps ten words of Mandarin memorised, it was a fresh start. Another new adventure. I loved new beginnings and was adept at sprinting from life. But in it all, I was erroneously believing that I was living life to the fullest. I was not living my best life but merely running from me. I couldn't face unpacking my authentic self for fear it was not aligned with the choices I'd made thus far. So I opted to unpack suitcases instead.

I can see my beleaguered Spirit Guides, guardian angels, ancestors, and all those universal forces who guide and protect me shaking their heads, placing bets on which way I will roll in this game of life as I blindly fumbled through it armed with knowledge but not wisdom. For I was lost. Utterly unconscious of what my life's purpose was. Blind to who I was. Spoilt and ego-driven in my relationships, wanting what I wanted, how I wanted it, when I wanted it, but failing to practise an iota of self-respect.

Had I paused, taken a breath, I would have been more discerning, more honest, and more aligned. I would have seen that both marriages were built on illusions. The illusion of the provider. The illusion of the protector. I was gullible. Plain and simple. But through this process and through these lessons, my resilience was fortified.

MORE LESSONS

The Universe taught me a third lesson, too: that it is easy to judge and hard to find true support. I learnt this quickly when my first divorce was finalised, and I showed up with my new fiancé. Things turned ugly quickly in the school playground with mothers who were previously my friends. Many turned their backs on me. I was no longer invited to dinner parties, and my children were excluded from playdates. My divorce was scandalous, and I was unapologetic.

Suddenly, the cracks in their own marriages were exposed, and I was the scapegoat who allegedly would now want to pursue their prize of a husband. As if! Of course, I had friends who upheld the sisterhood code and were fully aware that by isolating me, these other mothers were simply projecting their insecurities. After all, I had the gall to walk out of a marriage with three children under the age of twelve. Spats at the private school gates got ugly when one mother had the audacity to ask why Mark was collecting my children. After all, they were not even his. There were assumptions made that he was the provider now and that I had lured him in. I lost my shit. This kind of nastiness from the adults was unrelenting, but it only made me armour up to give zero fucks. All I was interested in was protecting my children from the nasty gossip and despicable behaviour towards them. But it still hurt. A lot.

Despite the turmoil and stigmas, my children excelled academically. The school gate whispers were, 'Why were these children not floundering academically under a broken home and a hoe for a mother?' This seemed to fuel even more jealousy from some quarters. I was not toeing the line as I should have. I should have kept my divorce under wraps or been more demure about the changes in my life. They had previously highlighted frustrations in some of their own partnerships and likely feared I would expose that. Clearly, they didn't know the integrity I upheld with my ardent girl code values. I was, however, good enough of a friend for them to dump their marital shit on, elicit advice, and then kick me to the curb. When I executed what they feared most, reassembling my own family unit and doing it right before their eyes, they were aghast and spat venomous words at my family. In hindsight, hurt people hurt people.

I still rocked up at school with a huge smile on my face while the mum who had asked me that question stepped out of her Porsche and couldn't manage a crack of a smile. Her face, akin to someone who had swallowed a wasp. I was happy getting out of my Mercedes in a state of bliss, coupled with an exhilarating sense of freedom rather than stuck in a cesspool of unhappiness, unwilling to break free. I had taken a risk and never played it safe.

Some risks pay off and some don't, but surely it's better to have risked and lived than to have not dared at all.

As the daily school grind continued, I felt more detached and there was an intense uneasiness within me. The daily routine of the carpool queues snaking along the designated lanes of the one-way system left me frustrated and questioning why I was here and was this really all I was meant to do. Was this my purpose? I vacantly observed the mothers boasting of their husbands working abroad, some complaining of being neglected, others putting on a brave face while their wretched kids threw satchels and rucksacks on the ground, screeching that they needed something NOW. Others still, showing off their newly acquired diamond ring or inviting one over for coffee to peruse their latest renovation or shitty purchase of some kind. An abyss of nothingness in which I didn't yet fit but which I was a part of. That's not to say all the mothers were pains up the arses. Absolutely not. There were some dear friends that I made along the way. I veered towards the ones who were honest and unafraid to point out the dullness of our lives, the challenges of our kids, and the loneliness we felt.

I laugh now at the ludicrous behaviours prevalent at private schools. Husbands cracking under the pressure of seeing who has the biggest dick by purchasing lavish cars for their wives to show off as they embark on more business trips and less family time. The Range Rover mum eyeing the Mercedes GLC mum against the Hyundai and Nissan mums. The puffing of fake boobs and filler lips at the school gates as the yoga and Pilates mums stand across from the Hermès and Louis Vuitton mums. Old money versus new money. On and on it goes. As the ancient Cree proverb states, 'Only when the last tree has withered, and the last fish has been caught, and the last river has been poisoned, will we realise we cannot eat money.' These folks devoured money and all the materialistic trappings involved.

Being ruled by a Venusian planet, I love nice things, and I've never believed spirituality and money are mutually exclusive. Money does not define who you are; it never has and it never will. Money is a mere energetic currency by which we live on this planet, but kindness and loyalty cost nothing. Yes, I enjoy a luxury car and am unapologetic about it. But as I sit behind the wheel, I am proud that no dickhead financed it, and I'm not held hostage to anyone because of it.

Disparaging comments about me coupled with backstabbing are nothing new, but I always believe in the glass being half full. For as much as there have been disappointments, there have been triumphs with friends who were loyal, sincere, and kind. This is the sisterhood of women who have built me up rather than break me down. Those who have shared what little they had with me when they had barely enough to feed themselves, and those who lent a shoulder to lean on and an ear to bend.

SPIRIT AND GUIDANCE
THROUGH IT ALL

Buddha said, 'Silence isn't empty. It's full of answers.' So what answers have I learnt? Well, that I'm a soul having a human experience. That when I pause and take a breath and stand silent and still, I hear and see that which normally eludes me. I learnt that I walked through life in a semi-conscious state and that, at times, I've walked through life completely unconscious, trapped in the cycle of attachment to material things and societal views and opinions.

Decades back (how annoying that I can say decades back), I was always searching for something more. I was what you'd call a dabbler. I dabbled in qigong when my firstborn was a toddler. I pondered tai chi, looked into Buddhism, veered towards Kabbalah. I was introduced to Osho Zen by the time my kids were in primary school. But never really stuck with anything. I was simply searching. Seeking answers and knowledge. I knew that something in my heart space needed filling. That *thingy* was craving nourishment.

Present day, I try to be more mindful. But let's be honest, I'm not present all of the time. Spirit knows I meander off in different directions constantly. So how do my Guides reach me? Well, I certainly do not, I repeat, do not meditate for hours. I simply cannot. Instead, they reach me through Spirit animals, through music, and through the bloody birds who chirp omens as loudly as they can. Oh, then there's all the bugs that abound with messages.

And there's even YouTube. No, I haven't lost my marbles. Often when I'm needing answers, I find them on YouTube. I call out to my angels if something perplexing comes up. I go onto YouTube, and what would you know—something pops onto my screen sending me in the direction I need to go. This is how it goes with faith. If you are open to it, it can reach you in the most bizarre ways. Would you believe me if I told you that I had not even known that tarot existed on YouTube a year ago. *That's odd*, you may say, but it's true. I asked for answers relating to this very book and voilà, opened up my laptop and the first thing on my screen directs me to a reader who leads me to my publisher. Strange but true. I put my music on shuffle and ask for answers, and the lyrics of songs guide me. I look up at the heavens seeking and am met with intuitive guidance. I have been fearful before, but now faith leads me. Both fear and faith require you to believe in that which is unseen. I choose the latter, as the path ahead is filled with promise, not doubt; with hope, rather than despondency; with courage and self-belief encapsulated in self-love. I no longer need validation from outside; I receive it from within the depths of my own soul.

Speaking of faith, I've also come to believe even more in past lives—I know that we have lived thousands of times before, not only here but elsewhere, and that our memories are charged from all these experiences. Reincarnation seems a no-brainer to me; if there's a Source so omnipotent and so powerful, why the hell would it limit its magick to only this plane. Dare to believe in the magnificence and the abundance of limitlessness and interconnectedness, for we are all a part of the same Source, a fragment of majesticness if we only choose to embrace this power.

Reincarnation is interpreted differently in different cultures. In Hinduism, it is that we are reborn so we can work off our karma, while in Buddhism, the intention behind the action determines your karma in the next life. In other beliefs, karma is merely payback: what you put out, you receive. I am certainly not an expert, but I do believe in the idea of working off your karma as you move forward towards your North Node and your dharma.

In my case, I am fulfilling my soul's purpose through my writing, through being of service in a bid to uplift others and through my story, hopefully, instilling hope. My purpose is to make others know that through the simple acknowledgement and gratitude for their breath, they are drawing closer to Spirit. That we all can be guided in the most wondrous of ways through a moment of silence. That whether you are religious or not, you are loved and have the ability to spread that love and light.

I also believe synchronicity and the orchestrating hand of the Universe led me to that patch of grass in my backyard. And as I stood grounding myself and looking towards the rocky outcrop of the mountain, everything changed.

Spirit—which you might call God or Source or Universe—speaks in a plethora of ways through music, through tarot, through deities, and through nature. In these, mysteries are unlocked and the celestial mysticism of the Universe is revealed. I have come to see that Spirit is everywhere, every day, in every breath of life. Look. Listen. Be still. You'll find Spirit there.

I've mentioned my archangels and guardian angel within my story. I've always believed in guardian angels. So much so that I walked brazenly into a church in Raynes Park, a suburb southwest of London, with my eldest daughter, who was a toddler at the time, and asked the vicar (it was Church of England) to please bless my daughter. Back then, I believed standing in a sacred space and using a conduit, such as a priest, to beckon the angels was necessary. He actually did. No questions asked. Now, that is my type of person of the cloth. Years later, David and I decided to have all the kids baptised so they could attend a Church of England school. I must confess, I did not particularly like the idea of having to attend church for months on end prior to their baptism. I was more interested in ordering the salmon for the party.

I've never been religious, although I was confirmed and attended Sunday school and then youth group. I found it amusing that my father would preach at the family church on a Sunday after being a bit of a drunk on a Saturday. His eldest brother was a preacher, too. My father hated his brother since he was his mum's favourite. But this was a family affair. The church was part of the Apostolic Unity congregation and encompassed a large community across South Africa.

Conditioning confirmed

Church was a painful and boring experience for me whenever I had to attend. It conjured up memories of a childhood of conformity where I was dragged every Sunday, forced to sing hymns horrendously out of tune, and wear hats. I had absolutely no idea what the hell the preachers were saying. Throughout my teen-age years, I often came in reeking of alcohol from clubbing and reminiscing of blurry fun times with my girlfriends. But still, I sat in the pew, barely able to keep my eyes open with my ears still ringing from the DJ tunes of the night before.

To me, religion is merely the same story of love and compassion and empathy told in a myriad of ways. It's Spirit's way of reaching a wide, diverse range of people. The sole purpose is to bring us all the way home. Back to the beginning. Back to God. Back to Source. Back to ourselves, our inner being of light and higher self-guidance via our intuition. Sadly, religion has been used to divide, to insti-gate wars, to assert control. Yet, at its core is one key element, and that is love. So how can those who are religious claim sovereignty over access to God and the magical lessons of the Cosmos when we are all made in the image of Source? We all have the innate ability to access the Power of the Universe, to converse with Source, to seek solace from Spirit, to call on our ancestors and our angels, for we are the Universe and the Universe is us.

The rules of the church were clear when I was young. Males and females were separated. Women had to cover their heads. I will never forget when my sister and my mother challenged this and walked into church, hatless. My father walked in and demanded to know what was happening and was met by a side-eye look from my mother. I clutched my little cream pearled bag, and in deathly silence, we walked to the car. Mother stepped out and walked into church as smartly dressed as she always was, plac-ing her handkerchief snappily back into her clutch purse as the gaping mouths of the congregation refused to shut. We usually sat right in front—God knows why. Right in front on the left-hand side with the other women. My brother would sit on the right side of the church near the front, while Dadda sat at the rear. The patriarchy was strong within the walls of worship.

Gasps continued to ripple through the congregation that day, and I realised that these man-made rules were in place to stranglehold that which is accessible to us all. It was silly. I was sure God didn't care if you came in shorts or straight from your shift as a nightwalker. All the judgements and rules were unnecessary. I didn't need to be confirmed to partake from the body and blood of Christ, which was merely a wafer and a sip of port.

In the process of rule-making, humankind forgot that Spirit exists in the trees and the oceans. We forgot that the wisdom of our ancestors and all our Indigenous tribes should be revived and revered. We forgot to express our simple gratitude for life. Look at the state of our planet. What we have manifested collectively is obvious. Our internal dialogue, our misalignment within ourselves, has revealed itself in the realities we now live within.

Sadly, in the pursuit of power and control by invading crusaders from various quarters, so many rituals and circles of connection were banished. Deities were deemed false gods. Corruption has distorted and denigrated the beauty of what was, what is, and what forever will be—a connected love—now known as God consciousness. Thankfully, moon rituals, tarot, and other forms of expression are now recognized to be enhancing our understanding of the flow of energy within and around us. All forms of our ancestral knowledge can help us all to move forward with mindful purpose, without judgement of one another.

I have seen these strange human dynamics of power and judgement play out many times in my life. While I was in Cape Town sitting in my comfortable security estate, another fire had just been doused in a nearby informal settlement. Thankfully, no one had lost their life, but possessions were destroyed. Although donations were generous by residents within the estate, the concept of Ubuntu was lost. *I am because you are. Your pain is my pain. Your success is my success.* We instead choose to ease our conscience and avoid facing our own selfish ways.

A charity drive within the largely white estate began. But as soon as the donation drive ended, the WhatsApp chat changed to the topic of unnecessary speed bumps in the estate, and how they were damaging the underside of people's luxury cars. Or how the 'no parking' demarcated red lines are inconveniences to visitors.

I had to shake my head in disbelief and resign myself to breathe. It wasn't so long ago that I laughed uncomfortably with those types of people. My one foot in and one foot out, but not standing for love. As I got busy in the local community, trying to fulfil a small portion of my soul's mission, I found it interesting that my faith was tested by a reborn Christian. She couldn't understand why I had not accepted JC into my life, why I practised yoga rather than church, why I lit sage rather than take communion, or why I combined Goddess Ishtar and Buddha and Lord Ganesha with Archangel Gabriel. I was grateful for her prayers, but I didn't appreciate the judgement. What was more important was the work we, as women, were trying to do during the pandemic for those adversely affected by Covid. Judgement had no place.

I tried to explain that, to me, spirituality was whatever makes me feel the sun from the inside out. Today it could be Hinduism, tomorrow Zen. Who knows? I like the combination of it all. My shrine holds both Buddha and Lord Ganesha, Goddess Lakshmi and Kali, bird feathers and angels, alongside candles, palo santo incense sticks, and bundles of sage, together with tarot cards and rose quartz. There's even a cross adjacent to some clear quartz. All faiths, all ancestral practices are beautiful to me. They are merely different ways leading us all to the same place. A place of Peace and Love.

Unfortunately, this Christian woman couldn't take it. While she questioned my lack of commitment to accepting JC as my Lord and Saviour and as the only access to Heaven, I tried to point out that God is not outside but within, that heaven is not among the clouds but on earth, and that beyond our realm there is so much more than we could even fathom. In the end, some of the best charitable work of feeding families was done by a spiritualist and a friend outside the woman's circle, who happened to be Muslim. The irony did not pass me by. All this talk of religion was exhausting and got us nowhere. So I, again, took a long breath.

I raised my kids to explore and find their own way. They've been inside some churches. They witnessed a congregant steal from the offering plate. This was my second attempt at entering the house of the Lord. Not good. They even heard a gospel band in a Beijing church (only foreigners are allowed to attend church) and incessantly complained how long that service was (three hours). They enjoyed spending time with my American Christian friend with Jewish heritage who had a charity in Langfang, China.

Rather than listen to people prattle on about God, she touched their hearts as she embodied all that God is. Love and kindness and a generous heart.

I've even lugged them to temples in Thailand, had them share Muslim prayers with friends, and exposed them to different faiths. They have seen me sage and palo santo the crap out of our house. One daughter converted to Judaism, one is into doing her bit for the planet rather than ascribing to a religion and politely says I'm eccentric while lighting her own incense. My eldest son dabbles and listens but is not convinced, while my youngest gives thanks to Spirit and practises his asana. Gratitude is all I ask that they practise daily. Whether they do or don't is for their soul to be accountable for. It is their wonderful journey to embrace, not mine.

I believe that what is more important than any church or any religion is our bodies, which are our temples, our vessels. It is this dense matter which we call our bodies that embody our emotions in physical form. When we feel good and are happy, our bodies align and are in top form and fit. When we are in a not-so-good space and we remain there, our bodies contain that emotion and are achy, our minds are garbled, and we feel and look like shit. We must align ourselves so we can hear Spirit. We must take care of ourselves to show gratitude for the bodies we possess. And we must be guardians of both our minds and our bodies to be the best version of ourselves and embody the highest form of self-love. Ultimately, by taking care of our inner selves, it will mirror on the outside, and as a result of our coming from a place of self-love and love for others, the vibrations of our planet will be raised, the frequency of *we* rather than *me* will infuse our societies and the Spirit of Ubuntu will prevail. We can only transmute the anger and hatred amongst our own kind by starting within. We must remember that we cannot change our circumstances by looking at others. I know now I have only me, and that's where I start. It is because of this belief that I qualified as a holistic wellness life coach and hope to impart some knowledge about how to get on the path, as it were. I encourage clients to lean into the mantra of Laozi which says, 'Mastering others is strength, but mastering yourself is true power.' I give thanks as I am light. It is in the now that the future is made. I have reaped what I have sowed. May the next generations understand the power they have.

How lucky am I that I found my heart chakra? That the *thingy* missing was the cracking open of my heart, the shedding of the pain in favour of joy, hope, and happiness. I feel at peace within the fluidity of time. I embrace my low and high vibrations, my tendency toward codependency at times and my independence at others. It is all about acceptance and self-love. The integration of my darkness and my light. The progression forward is bumpy, but still, it must flow.

CHAPTER 8

Healing

#lovingmeafterwe

'You will suffer many defeats in life, but never let yourself be defeated.'

MAYA ANGELOU

MY JOURNEY IN LIFE HAS SEEN ME WANDERING AIMLESSLY FOR a long time, like a boat without a rudder. I've always felt different. A dreamer. A bit of a circus traveller, as Mamma said. My restlessness and the 'upping and going constantly' was a foreign concept to Mamma, who was from a generation that believed putting down roots was vital to stability. Deviating from this was shameful. But to me, home was where my family was. I always had my kids by my side. Even romantic weekends included them. I have a memory of an elaborate dinner in the middle of a forest

185

with my three children also sitting at the table with us. I wanted them to see that I would never abandon them, though I think sometimes they still felt abandoned. And just like it was not my burden to fix David or Mark, neither is it my responsibility to fix my children. I can only be a guide, and whatever judgement they may have of me, from that I must detach. For their truth is not mine. All varied perceptions and viewpoints in which different experiences and emotions are anchored.

Subconsciously, the opinions of others and outdated traditions influenced many of my choices. Yet externally, I was rebellious. Unabashed and open about my struggles as a mum and a wife. Opinionated on why women should not put up with controlling partners who try to undermine their worth. I could see it plainly in others, yet in my own circumstances, I was blind.

How easily I attached shame to all my mistakes or, rather, learning experiences. I was critical of myself as a mother, and my children sometimes criticised me as a mum, too. This is a bitter pill to swallow, but everything circles back to my own value and how I measure myself—even against the opinions of offspring. I tried to give them what I thought was the best I had to offer. My Mamma, undoubtedly, had the same intentions—doing the best that she knew how. That's how the circle of life works.

As mentioned earlier in my memoir, before healing commenced, I was a wanderer in every way. I enjoyed morphing, both my names and abodes. If I fancied changing countries today, I would up and leave. A new name or a variation of my name was a fresh beginning, similar to a new country signifying a fresh start. I have moved more than twenty times in my life, encompassing several homes, cities, and countries as mentioned before, but none of this quelled the restlessness within my soul.

Previously, to feel alive, I moved spontaneously and sporadically which initiated my precious kids and I into adventure after adventure. It meant us all adjusting to new surroundings, delving into new friendships, getting to know new neighbourhoods, and it meant doing it all together. This subconsciously made me feel secure and alive. It gave meaning to my physical life and injected excitement into a life devoid of consistent spiritual gratitude for where I was. I chased desire after desire which can never be fulfilled. For such was the nature of my earthly desire: to pursue either emotional or material fulfilment externally but to neglect internal spiritual purpose, and as we saw throughout my book, painfully try to find that *thingy* that was amiss within my life.

Living for my children gave my life meaning. Striving to make them happy gave me joy. Always external fulfilment in a bid to extinguish that *thingy* that was elusive. I was not able to be nor recognise my truth and so could not identify my authentic power within. I chased feeling alive rather than enjoying each moment and, in doing so, failed to live each day with a thankful heart.

I was quite adept at running, wouldn't you agree? But I couldn't outrun myself.

The truth is that the attempt, as you now know, to respire my marriage through quenching our wanderlust, even with our children in tow, was futile. In reality, I was expertly sprinting from myself, lost and without identity. Others saw me as confident, adventurous, a bit of an eccentric, and certainly fearless—happy-go-lucky. Partially true, but as perceptions go, it's only a perceived truth. I was, indeed, happy most of the time, but there was always that *thingy* missing. That *thingy* you don't even know you have, that *thingy* that hasn't got a name but you know something is amiss. Rather than running towards myself, I was running away, unaware that years would pass and nothing would still the restlessness and that *thingy* amiss would remain until I stopped and took a breath and fearlessly decided to face the emptiness within.

I would feverishly redecorate every house—a systematic budding climax of each move. Even just before the explosive collapse of my second marriage, I was ripping out kitchens and redoing floors in a bid to deflect from my pain and fill my life with pointless tasks. The most important task, though, was the internal discovery of my purpose on this planet. The purpose of my life. I had no choice but to stand in the stillness of what the fuck now—what now after four kids and two marriages and an estranged family? What now, Spirit?

Now was the time to rebuild in honesty and truth and to discard the lies and excuses that I had carefully orchestrated around myself to 'protect' myself from the brutality of it all—-that no one would come save me. That it was up to me to save myself. The only way I could do that was to call upon the Universe for guidance. For only in the eye of the storm, so to speak, did I acknowledge that Spirit was there all along, and I was never alone. Only during my moments of tears and silence and more tears and stillness and yet more tears and serenity did I understand that to feel supported, I had to start supporting myself; to feel love I had to start loving myself. That I had to nurture myself in order to nurture a relationship with Spirit/Source, and no one and nothing else mattered. For only through this unravelling and subsequent tenderness towards myself was I able to garner guidance from the Universe. And only through being grateful for its divine interventions and redirections in my life did it reveal itself more and more to me.

Even my laser focus on my children was unhealthy. I put all my energy in building their belief in themselves, and it was my mission to enhance their sense of adventure as my own childhood was devoid of travel. Despite not having the luxuries and privileges during my own childhood, my parents instilled in me an unwavering belief in my abilities to conquer whatever I wanted. I had resilience and I wanted my kids to have this innate quality as well. All this newness when entering new cities was refreshing, exciting, and untainted. It certainly required resilience over fear.

The moves allowed tainted hurt and broken dreams to be left behind in former homes. The arguments with my spouse and the snide remarks dumped in the old neighbourhood while the new foreign environment burst with promise of new hope, new dreams, and new beginnings. But these new beginnings often lost their sparkle as old problems and challenges resurfaced. Different location, same shit. Eventually, I had no choice, albeit decades later to change from within as changing locations was clearly not the answer to the quizzical puzzle of my life.

I have learnt much from my childhood wounds, my relationships, my friendships, and my marriages. The learning continues as the struggle to always change perspective daily forces me to balance my emotions. To deal with them patiently and compassionately but not identify with them. The process is ongoing. Some days, I wake up and feel like shit, but before that shitty feeling threatens to ruin my entire day and week—before it snowballs into feisty confrontations, I face my uncomfortable feelings in stillness. I breathe. Sometimes it works. Other times it doesn't, in which case I work out or stretch or listen to music. Or I yell. Dramatics aside, it was well overdue that I had to take stock of my life.

A stern look at myself with kindness, I had to face my role in it all. My shadow self was unearthed as I looked at not what went wrong in both marriages, but rather, where did *I* go wrong because both men were not my typical type, so how come I had veered so far off course from who I was and what I truly wanted. And even if my partners fulfilled all I demanded from them, my own lack of self-love would have yielded the same outcome. An unfulfilled me in an unfulfilled relationship living an unfulfilled life.

When I chose my first hubby, I had not taken enough time out to consider who I was. At twenty-two, I hadn't even garnered the tools to understand feelings and how emotions have to be tempered with logic, hence the blessing of both heart and brain. I never understood what loving myself truly meant. I chose to let emotion cloud my judgement. I let fairy tales infiltrate my brain. I let the romance of travelling sweep me off my feet.

I convinced myself that this is how it should be. He was no alpha male. His divine masculinity and femininity unbalanced, mirroring my own imbalance. Both wounded people required nurturing. My fear of abandonment, coupled with my urge to make things better, was the foundation of those first nuptials with David.

With Mark, I tried to balance out the laid-back attitude of David with the assertiveness of Mark, but as I now know, you cannot get the balance in anything—especially in relationships—by looking outward. Partners cannot rectify imbalances for the imbalances were deep within me. My reality was my manifestation. What I lacked, I sought from them, but I would never find it as my internal state was mirrored in that which I sought. The missing *thingy* that's a fuzzy ball of a number of things like love and acceptance, recognition, and validation. But only I could fill that gap; neither one of them could fulfil that need. I lacked self-love and firm boundaries. I couldn't discern between love and neediness, between healthy and toxic. I was consumed by making it work and bottling my pain. I chose to nurture and fix a thirteen-year marriage and then a seven-year marriage. I needed to accept and acknowledge me first. This was the key.

I believed love was to give and give some more and that to be selfish was wrong. How in the world could I ever comprehend self-love since self-love is to be unapologetically selfish of one's self, one's boundaries, and one's needs. Society has successfully cloned women into being the nurturers, which encompasses self-denial of our own needs and desires in favour or dishing out that love to those who need it. I witnessed my mum do it for years and years; she still does—to this day—a product of her environment, as am I. **I inhale and accept who I am. As I release the breath on the exhale, I accept who I'm about to become.**

Before all the pain and cheating and all the broken heartedness, I was driven by ego.

Now don't get me wrong. Ego is good. Ego is what motivates us. Our human state is driven by our ego but when it overrides everything, we become insatiable. We need to be heart-centred when making decisions in life and in love; and even then, it has to be balanced with logic. Everything is duality and the integration thereof.

Years after Dadda died, Mamma mentioned, in passing, how Dadda was impressed that David 'hung up his work suit and then got changed to play with the children for a little bit.' Dadda didn't even know him that well yet. Like me, we all operated from a value system of skewed traits and morals imprinted in our human frames through conditioning.

Even as I reflect, I'm in disbelief. I think, *Crikey, Jax, take a breath—breathe—what was the rush to marry again? And why to someone the exact opposite in character to your first husband?* I went from cerebral, emotionally unattached, and unavailable to brawny, emotionally unattached, and unavailable. You cannot make this shit up. I had this deeply engraved framework etched in my muggle frame that I needed to belong in a family. That I had to create this family as only then would I have honoured myself and my children with stability. I did not believe I was enough.

This insecurity of not being enough saw me try to force traditional values onto my unhappy existence. I wanted the kids to have a father in their lives as I did. Conveniently, I erased all the pain and the tumultuousness of my own parents' marriage. My mother, a true martyr, stayed. My domineering father controlled everything—emotionally abusive coupled with being a provider. Their frustration both apparent throughout the marriage. My own frustrations, apparent in both marriages, and still I continued unconsciously—far too fearful to make a conscious decision that this was not the life I wanted. The life I wanted did not fit in with what was expected.

One thing I did admire of my parents was their loyalty to each other when any outsider dared to attack either one of them. I admired this loyalty and probably craved this from subsequent partners but soon realised that both husbands capitulated under the presence of my Boeta which I tagged, rightly or wrongly, as weakness. Never had I ever been so close and personal to witness how wealth and power can make men cower and feel less than next to him. How egos battle it out and how money and power always won.

In essence, the framework into which I chose to be born was fucked up but marginally less fucked up than other scenarios. So, again, I can be nothing but truly grateful. For the more dysfunctional, the greater the tools of learning.

MARITAL LESSONS

Intrinsically, I believed that my children would benefit from a traditional family. I believed this so fervently that I went from one marriage to the next with just a slight two-year break in between. Intuitively, I knew I probably shouldn't have married, and had I been in tune with omens, I would have seen the oh-so-obvious signs my angels were giving me.

When I look at the circumstances surrounding both marriages, I am flabbergasted at not seeing the signposts from above.

Marriage number one. The venue we chose was not legit and they stole our entire deposit days before the wedding. This transpired for us directly linked to my naivety and wanting to please an aunt by using her 'connection.' A sum of money that took months to save was gone. We were scammed. Had I been listening to my guardian angels, I would have paused, taken a breath, and reconsidered the whole marriage shebang even though invitations were sent out. I would have faced my biggest fear of telling them I had a bun in the oven, and I would've realised dear David was not ready for another marriage, never mind fatherhood. I could've done it on my own, but fear and the illusion of marriage took over, and as they say, the rest is history. At least we got married in an auspicious year when the South African rainbow nation voted for the first time.

Marriage number two. The initial yacht that was booked had engine trouble. Another obvious omen. My guardian angels assessed that it was best to give her the most obvious nudge this time 'round—surely, she'll get it. Nope, I didn't. I was too busy living out my dream of a yacht wedding and it was bloody worth it. Two yachts were used, one for a trip into the open Atlantic waters for the vows, the other for the jovial party. I skedaddled into a second marriage, still completely oblivious to who the hell I was and what I was seeking.

I created my own reality within my matrix so no one is to blame for how my life transpired because of my choices. I had lessons to learn throughout and am thankful that where I was once blind, I now see that the Universe always had a plan and always had my back. All I needed to do was sashay slower and be open to the whispers of the infinite. I'm slow on the uptake, but eventually I got it.

There is solace to be had in knowing that I am linked to Source, to God, to the Universe and that you and I are gods or goddesses incarnate. We are made in the image of Source, and that is bloody phenomenal when you realise the infinite possibilities and power that comes with this. Religion, as mentioned before, never sat well with me because I always felt restricted, but exercising my freedom of choice to honour Spirit how I wish has brought me inner peace and clarity. Spirit or God or Source is not outside. It is within. I am the ultimate creation that holds the power of energy, of choice, and of manifestation. I can create my heaven on earth. We all can. After all, we are co-creators.

That *thingy* is no longer missing as I let go of both judgement and expectations. Cutting free from all the what-ifs and shoulda, coulda, wouldas of life. Gone. Just emptiness remains. An emptiness that fills the gap in my soul.

GETTING HONEST WITH ME

Healing from the most recent disaster has taken years. I've been celibate for nearly three and a half years now. People ask if this is out of choice. Obviously, it's a choice. Not to toot my own horn, but it's not like I'm short of suitors. But an angel spreads her wings and not her legs (wink-wink). That's my latest banter when I'm on dating apps. Yep, I'm trying to get out there again and am cautiously optimistic. But I honestly don't have time for any bullshit, so my authentic self often scares them off. I'm trying to be the flower rather than the bee. The flower waits for the bee to come to it; in the meantime I'm just soaking up the sun.

During my healing, I have heeded my inner voice. I haven't needed sex to feel desired or valued, so I didn't go after it. I steered clear of any emotional intimacy, too. I only had enough emotional reserves for me. I turned inward, driving all the energy I had towards myself. I know I can only be intimate if I am emotionally connected. No shame in my game nor in anyone else's choices. Different strokes for different folks, as the saying goes. Healing for me has involved unpacking my life. It required me to create my own kintsugi love story with myself. To rebuild myself.

I needed to accept all of me, and the Universe delivered blow after blow so that I would succumb and crack open. When there was nothing more that could be pummelled out of me, all that was left for me to do was drop to my knees and lift my hands to the heavens. At that point of empty, I was transformed into a vacant vessel ready to receive. In my acceptance, I see I am both darkness and light. I am a being of duality. A soul. An energetic force in human form exuding both dark and light characteristics—for without each other, neither exists. As I see it, darkness is to be understood, accepted, and transmuted into light, to be acknowledged before it consumes me.

At many points in my life, many things consumed me. One glass of wine turning into a bottle. One slice of cake turning into an addiction to sugar. One negative comment, turning into a feeling of defeat. The list is endless. My emotions still rise and fall, but

I now know it's my duty to tap in, to balance my inner states of being and to understand that I cannot allow people, circumstances, and things on the outside to influence my inner well-being. When we have control of our inner emotional state, then we have a choice to descend or transcend.

To tap in, I have learnt to breathe. To pause. We all need to learn to do this. Do it with me now. Just breathe. Inhale deeply and hold. Then exhale. Inhale deeply through the nose and hold, then exhale through the mouth. Think of nothing but the breath. Be thankful for life.

And remember to simplify. I learnt the importance of simplicity in Thailand. I found a sense of peace watching the poorest of poor families simply embracing life. No material trappings. No resentment. No complaints. Just embracing each moment and performing daily chores mindfully with gratitude for the blessing of life itself.

I no longer feel guilty for not wanting to attend church services since my early twenties and accept that I have always been drawn to Spirit in ways I could previously never explain. I loved the esoteric and mysticism of the Universe even before I had a name for it. From a young age, I loved gazing at the angel paintings in my grandmother's darkened room, dreamily taken to a place of peace. Seraphims and cherubims, majestic amongst the fluffy clouds and pastel blue skies. I remember as a young girl always staring at the stars and feeling the magic of it all, wishing to be there.

We are all linked to Source and have a purpose to fulfil, to leave this planet slightly better than we found it. May your flicker become a flame to uplift humanity. Whether it's saving the planet, saving the kids, or a kind deed towards a stranger. I have benefited from remembering the African Ubuntu saying, 'I am because you are.' Collectively a change is made. Societies did not become what they are on their own. We are all responsible.

Acknowledging that there is always someone better off or worse off than you can instantly put your life in perspective. It's also tremendously helpful to remember that not everyone is going to like you. Not everyone vibes at your frequency, and that is neither good nor bad. It just is what it is. Just like a sunflower is yellow—not red or brown or black—it's just yellow because it is. Over the years, I have embraced all aspects of what makes me me. Both high and low vibrations. Sometimes I'm fearful, codependent, and needy, and at other times, I'm self-sufficient, fearless, and independent. These are all parts of who I am. I practise gratitude and acknowledge grace daily. This is my path. No more running from me. Just standing still and being SILENT. Silent = Listen (rearrange the letters).

It's taken me decades to discern when to be a fool and when to be an empress. A fool takes those leaps of faith in the tarot. There's a time for that. An Empress encompasses all the Queens, and she sits on her throne, confident and discerning. Her power lies in her ability to know when to leap. When to love. When to be logical. She follows her intuition and has firm boundaries in place that nourish her SELF but do not barricade her heart. She knows when to concentrate on her coins and when to play, when to be logical, and when to be emotional. I now understand it is imperative to encompass all of these aspects of myself, but most importantly, I understand that the practice of *doing* daily unlocks it all. As the cliché goes, consistency is key. I am proof that in the daily practice of gratitude and silence, you will find the golden light of self-love. A product of this self-love is my peak physical transformation, the external manifestation of my body being a temple in honour of Source. My glow-up is a result of my flow. No shortcuts, no quick fixes.

Before my healing, I had forgotten that I descended from a line of chiefs destined for greatness. Forgotten how to tap into Spirit. Forgotten that in silence I'm able to heed my soul. Now I choose to no longer crack on blindly in life. I choose to see grace.

Perspective is my key. When things go wrong, it hurts like hell, but perspective is what gets you out of the slump. Like the hangman in the tarot, perspective changes everything. I took my perceived hardships and used them as lessons. I went inward and asked myself what I learnt. What won't I do again? What can I share with others from my experiences? I harnessed my ability to learn from my perceived failure rather than fester in a cesspool of disappointment.

In the end, only your heart knows the divine truth. Allow it to open and feel all the glory of emotions. The majesty of being broken brings about the incredible ability to rise. The chasm of a broken heart opened me up to the process of infinite learning and healing so I could fill up with joy. The divinity of darkness forged a way to know I am indeed light and divinity itself.

CHAPTER 9

Another Pause, Another Breath

#staywokeandbreathe

'The secret of change is to focus all your energy not on fighting the old, but on building the new.'

SOCRATES

PERHAPS READING MY BOOK HAS TRIGGERED UNCOMFORTABLE realisations for you, just like writing it unearthed moments of harsh truths and periods of pause for me. It was hard having to face my own moments of martyrdom, similar to that of Mamma, control issues like Dadda, ego issues akin to Boeta, hurt and resentment like that of Sis. But the shadow work was meaningful, the crying was cathartic, and the purging brought much needed humility and inner peace.

I have learnt so much on my journey amid divorce and codependency, so much surrounding my judgements of myself and others. I have finally understood the wisdom in letting go. I've learnt much about my periods of arrogance and assumption, my moments of overextended energy, and my methods of control. My growth relied on raw honesty, an openness, a willingness to entertain different perspectives on truth, whether it be my truth or someone else's truth. As I navigated home inward, I realised there is but one ultimate truth, and it resides in I AM. I am the choices I make. I am the circumstances I find myself in.

Ah yes, choice. Oh, that ultimate little freedom we often take for granted and mindlessly exercise. That delightful option that the Universe gives us each day. Choice is what decides our karmic path. Our ornament of grace is our voice, intentions, and actions. These combined tools certainly defined and decided my path, however unconsciously I used them. They carved my road in life. All the while, omnipotent Spirit, my ancestors, and angels sat back and observed what transpired until they witnessed that I was way, way off course, wishing for better, yet wasting opportunities to evolve. I imagine how they put their exasperated head in their hands and watched me being a silly cow going 'round and 'round, doing the same thing in the same rodeo with another cowboy and expecting a different result with the same stank attitude towards myself.

Finally, reeling in the absurdity of my glorious pain and demise, I was shown the connectedness of it all—my connectedness to you. The internal fight within me danced around my head as I felt entitled to this grief, anger, loss, and sadness. Yes, I was allowed to feel all these emotions because it is part of my experience here on earth, but I was not entitled to blame. I created my own bullshit, and it was up to me to create a new outcome. I have only one life to live, and I want to live it fulfilling my soul's purpose. Ultimately, I had to choose me. And I'll never abandon myself again.

Now I choose to view my life from a higher perspective. For I am in this world but not of this world. I have lived millennia before, and my soul's purpose is to evolve and then to return home. Back home to Source, the Alpha and the Omega, the beginning and the end, the place of neutrality where nothing is judged as good or bad but simply is.

The omnipotent presence of Spirit is everywhere and in every day. The rapturous celestial entourage of the Universe speaks to me in an array of ways—sometimes through the music of the Indigenous Native American tribes and sometimes via the birds or in the form of various Spirit animals. At other times, Source speaks through deities or through the touch of a tree or the smell of a flower or the spray of the ocean. Seeing the beauty of nature allows me to see myself. Honouring and respecting nature allows me to respect myself. Witnessing the intricacies of nature allows me to acknowledge the same within myself. My physical transformation has been tremendous, and my attitude to my physical body is one of joy and gratitude.

Thankfully, I've come this far in my journey still believing in love. A giddy, passionate, and exhilarating type of love. A soul connection that is deep, a love that is wild, and a man that combines both the elements of thug and Buddha. A Normani and Cardi B Wild Side kinda love. But now I know Spirit has to be central in the union, something all my previous relationships lacked.

CHOOSING LIFE

Daily, I ask that Spirit, my Angels, my Ancestors, and Spirit Animals intervene in my life for my highest good so that I may fulfil my soul's purpose, my dharma. What does this mean? This means I *choose to* allow the Divine to place obstacles where it sees fit and to clear the path where it deems fit so that I may not veer from the path of connectedness. Part of my life's purpose is this book, and for that, I am grateful.

Gratitude coupled with forgiveness of self has freed me. Because I can forgive myself, I do not seek forgiveness from my children any longer. I can work at always making sure my cup of love towards myself is full. In this way, I honour me. By honouring myself, I am honouring Spirit, my ancestors, and life. To honour life, I also have to honour the body that allows me to walk through life. I no longer walk in fear or anxiety about tomorrow as I accept, through faith, that I am divinely protected by the grace that the Universe has so lovingly bestowed on me and my family. Through self-love, I can heal ancestral wounds because I know now I AM enough. I AM never alone.

All through life I have tried to harness an attitude of gratitude, always digging deep to try and cultivate happiness even inside dysfunctional circumstances. I always knew it was up to me, myself, and I. These days, protecting my energy is vital, and my boundaries are firmer. Although I follow my path of spirituality with passion, it does not mean I'm all about light and love. I once saw a quote that said 'I am Spiritual with a hint of Tupac.' This reflects more of what I'm about.

My kindness was often mistaken for weakness, but my children can attest that I can be fearsome to authority if someone I love is threatened. The same energy now applies to my well-being. I'm happy to take a deep inhale and exhale and still tell you to fuck right off if you push me too far. Until then, I am all Nama-fucking-ste. This may not sit well with many who consider them-selves 'on the path,' but no one has exclusivity on spirituality. We all have our own personal journeys to make. What I know is that Spirit has my back and yours, too.

Although I am but a leaf on an enormous tree of life, I am still part of the tree. No more and no less.

ENDING AT THE NUMBER NINE

Serendipitously, my life has been condensed into nine chapters. The number 9 signifies both endings and beginnings—being the last of the single-digit cardinal numbers. This number is revered in Hinduism and is considered a divine number, as it represents the end of a cycle and is the number of Brahma, the Creator. In Christianity, it is believed that Jesus died at the 9th hour when he was crucified, and his death represents a resurrection for believers, as he died for humanity's sins. In the Baha'i faith, it symbolises culminations and is a sacred digit. The number 108 is also sacred in Buddhism and can be reduced to 9 (add 1 + 0 + 8 = 9). In Islam, 9 is also a special number, and the holy month of Ramadan is the 9th month of the calendar. The 9th day of the Chinese New Year is the birthday of the Jade Emperor, ruler of Heaven and Earth worshipped by Taoists. A woman is pregnant for 9 months before giving birth to new life.

The list is endless, but I'd like to conclude with two important interpretations of the number. Angel number 9 is about universal love, soul purpose, and being of service. In numerology, it is a number of forgiveness and compassion on the one hand but can still hold resentment and arrogance on the other. The duality of this reflects the duality of life. I cannot wish away moments of my ego-driven behaviour, but I can see them as opportunities to listen to my heart and choose a new way. To accept the perfectness of imperfection. To accept the truth of life. To be wise, as Rumi says, 'Yesterday I was clever, so I wanted to change the world. Today I am wise, so I am changing myself.'

Acknowledgements

I AM SO GRATEFUL TO THE SCRIBE TEAM WHO SUPPORTED and believed in me and who were an integral part of my soul tribe, collaborating with me to see my vision come to fruition. From the attentive copy editors and proofreaders to the design, graphics, and layout team. The mutual energy was one of love. Special thanks to my lovely Publishing Manager, Katie Villalobos, who ignited in me sparks of sisterhood throughout the process. To the Editor, John Mannion, who clarified so much in a kind and supportive manner, to the Cover Designer, Teresa Muniz, and Title Workshopper, Skyler Gray, just pure joy and magick in the creative process, and last but not least, the warm Erin Michelle Sky, the Back Cover Copywriter, who added her sparkle to the overall bliss of making this book possible. Thank you.

Songs for your soul:

- 'Give Thanks' and 'I am Light' are two songs by India Arie

- 'Circle of Light' and 'Amazing Grace' by Walela

- 'Spirit Mountain' by Andrew Vasquez

- 'Let Us All Come Together' by Joe Tonhonnie Jr.

- 'Seteng Sediba' by Soweto Gospel Choir

Lightworkers on YouTube that may be of help to guide you on your path:

- Baba Jolie guided messages

- CAN be the light

- Soulful Revolution

- Eat Read Love Inc

- Saltwater Heals Tarot

- Your Sacred Scribe Tarot

Acknowledgements

- Mermaid Scales Tarot

- Patrizia 1111

- Golden Era

Divinity defined

Starched ribbons and anglaised socks

1994: South Africa's first all-race elections
(Photo credit: George Hallett)

Lightning Source UK Ltd.
Milton Keynes UK
UKHW010640100622
404199UK00003B/72/J